Writing Empirical Research Reports

A Basic Guide for Students of the Social and Behavioral Sciences

Third Edition

Fred Pyrczak

California State University, Los Angeles

Randall R. Bruce

Editorial Consultant

Pyrczak Publishing

P.O. Box 39731 • Los Angeles, CA 90039

Editorial assistance provided by Brenda Koplin, Sharon Young, Elaine Fuess, and Cheryl Alcorn.

Cover design by Robert Kibler and Larry Nichols.

Printed in the United States of America.
10 9 8 7 6 5 4 3 2   DOC   06 05 04 03 02 01 00

ISBN 1-884585-24-8

Table of Contents

Notes:

Introduction to the Third Edition

This book presents guidelines frequently followed by writers of empirical research reports. The guidelines describe the types of information that should be included, how this information should be expressed, and where various types of information should be placed within a research report.

Students whose professors require them to write research-based term papers that resemble journal articles will find this book useful. The exercises at the end of each chapter are designed for their use. Graduate students who are writing theses and dissertations will find that most of the guidelines also apply to their writing. Interspersed throughout the text are pointers for such students. Finally, students who are writing research proposals will also find that most of the guidelines apply to their writing.

What This Book Will *Not* Do for You

This book is not a traditional style manual that prescribes mechanical details such as how to cite references, the forms for levels of headings, typing requirements, and so on. A number of excellent style manuals, including the *Publication Manual of the American Psychological Association*, already cover these matters. Neither will you find here a discussion of the mechanics of standard English usage; it is assumed that you have already mastered these. Finally, it is assumed that you already selected an important research topic, applied sound research methods, and analyzed the data. Thus, these topics are not covered.

Cautions in Using This Book

The guidelines presented in this book are based on generalizations that we reached while reading extensively in journals in the social and behavioral sciences. If you are a student using this book in a research class, your professor may ask you to ignore or modify some of the guidelines you will find here. This may occur for two reasons. First, as a learning experience, your professor may require you to do certain things that go beyond the preparation of a paper for possible publication. For example, we suggest that the literature review for a journal article should usually be highly selective; your professor may have you write a more extensive literature review, which would indicate that you know how to locate literature and demonstrate your breadth of knowledge of the research topic. Second, as in all types of writing, there is a certain amount of subjectivity concerning what constitutes effective writing; even experts differ. Fortunately, these differences are less pronounced in scientific writing than in many other types.

Experienced writers may violate many of the guidelines presented in this book and still write effective research reports that are publishable. Beginners are encouraged to follow the guidelines rather closely until they have mastered the art of scientific writing.

Where to Begin in This Book

For a quick overview of five fundamental principles for effective research writing, begin with Appendix B, *Thinking Straight and Writing That Way*. Then read Chapter 1, which will help you formulate a simple research hypothesis.

About the Third Edition

All the guidelines that were in the first edition are included in this one. You will find that many of the examples that illustrate the guidelines have been updated with newer examples dealing with contemporary issues. In addition, Guideline 10.8 in Chapter 10 has been added as well as an entirely new chapter on writing reports of qualitative research (Chapter 12).

Acknowledgements

The authors are grateful to Dr. Dean Purcell of Oakland University, who provided many helpful comments on the first edition of this book. Dr. Robert Morman of California State University, Los Angeles, provided many suggestions on the drafts of both the first and second editions. Any errors, of course, remain the responsibility of the authors.

Chapter 1

Writing Simple Research Hypotheses

In a single sentence, a simple research hypothesis describes the results that a researcher expects to find. In effect, it is a prediction. The following are guidelines for writing this type of hypothesis.

➤ Guideline 1.1   A simple research hypothesis should name two variables and indicate the type of relationship expected between them.

In Example 1.1.1, the variables are "psychomotor coordination" and "self-esteem." The researcher expects to find higher self-esteem among individuals who have more psychomotor coordination and lower self-esteem among those who have less coordination. Note that the word "positive" may be substituted for "direct" without changing the meaning of the hypothesis.

Example 1.1.1
There is a direct relationship between level of psychomotor coordination and degree of self-esteem.

In Example 1.1.2, "length of light deprivation" is a stimulus or *independent variable*, which will be manipulated by the researcher. The hypothesis suggests that some rats will be deprived of light longer than others will. The second variable is "performance in a maze task," which is an outcome or *dependent variable*. The hypothesis indicates that the researcher expects to find more light deprivation associated with poorer maze performance.

Example 1.1.2
Among rats, length of light deprivation from birth is inversely associated with performance in a maze task.

Example 1.1.3 also contains an independent variable—the type of paper given to teachers. The anticipated relationship of this variable to the willingness of teachers to accept learning disabled students is clear in the hypothesis. Their willingness to have learning disabled students in their classrooms is the dependent variable.

Example 1.1.3

Teachers who are given a paper containing practical tips on teaching learning disabled students will be more willing to have such students in their classrooms than teachers who are given a theoretical paper on learning disabilities.

In Example 1.1.4, two variables are named, but the expected relationship between them is not stated. The Improved Version of Example 1.1.4 makes it clear that the researcher believes that those with more free-floating anxiety have less ability to form friendships.

Example 1.1.4

College students differ in their levels of free-floating anxiety, and they differ in their ability to form friendships.

Improved Version of Example 1.1.4

Among college students, there is an inverse relationship between level of free-floating anxiety and ability to form friendships.

Note that in the Improved Version of Example 1.1.4, the word "negative" could be substituted for "inverse" without changing the meaning of the hypothesis.

➢ Guideline 1.2   When a relationship is expected only in a particular population, reference to the population should be made in the hypothesis.

In Example 1.2.1, young children are identified as the researcher's population of interest.

Example 1.2.1

Among young children, there is a direct relationship between level of psychomotor coordination and degree of self-esteem.

➢ Guideline 1.3   A simple hypothesis should be as specific as possible, yet expressed in a single sentence.

The Improved Version of Example 1.3.1 is more specific than the original because the meanings of "computer literacy" and "computer use" are indicated in the improved version.

Example 1.3.1

There is a direct relationship between administrators' computer literacy and their computer use.

Improved Version of Example 1.3.1

Among administrators, there is a direct relationship between the amount of training they have had in the use of computers and the number of administrative tasks they perform using computers.

Likewise, the Improved Version of Example 1.3.2 is more specific than the original version because the improved version indicates that "effectiveness" will be measured in terms of employees' perceptions of leadership qualities. Also, the improved version is more specific because it indicates that two types of administrators will be compared.

Example 1.3.2

Administrators who provide wellness programs for their employees project positive effectiveness.

Improved Version of Example 1.3.2

Administrators who provide wellness programs for their employees receive higher employee ratings on selected leadership qualities than administrators who do not provide wellness programs.

A certain amount of subjectivity enters into the decision on how specific to make a hypothesis. It is usually not possible to provide full definitions of all terms in the single sentence that states a hypothesis. Complete definitions should be provided elsewhere in a research report. Guidelines for writing definitions are presented in Chapter 6.

➢ Guideline 1.4   If a comparison is to be made, the elements to be compared should be stated.

Comparisons start with terms such as "more," "less," "higher," and "lower." Be sure to complete any comparisons you start with these terms. The comparison that is started in Example 1.4.1 is not complete, forcing the reader to make an assumption about the group(s) to which the low-achieving students will be compared. The improved versions are superior because they complete the comparison that starts with the word *more*. Note that the improved versions illustrate that the comparison can be completed in more than one way, clearly showing that the original version is vague.

Example 1.4.1

Low-achieving primary-grade students are more dependent on adults for psychological support.

Improved Versions of Example 1.4.1

Low-achieving primary-grade students are more dependent on adults for psychological support than average achievers.

Low-achieving primary-grade students are more dependent on adults for psychological support than high achievers.

Low-achieving primary-grade students are more dependent on adults for psychological support than average and high achievers.

➢ Guideline 1.5   Because most hypotheses deal with the behavior of groups, plural forms should usually be used.

In Example 1.5.1, the terms "nurse" and "her level" are singular. The problem has been corrected in the improved version by substituting the terms "nurses" and "their level." Note that in the Improved Version of Example 1.5.1, the sex-role stereotype regarding nurses has been eliminated. Of course, it is important to avoid sex-role stereotyping throughout research reports.

Example 1.5.1

There is a direct relationship between a nurse's participation in administrative decision making and her level of job satisfaction.

Improved Version of Example 1.5.1

There is a direct relationship between nurses' participation in administrative decision making and their level of job satisfaction.

➤ Guideline 1.6 A hypothesis should be free of terms and phrases that do not add to its meaning.

The Improved Version of Example 1.6.1 is much shorter than the original version, yet its meaning is clear.

Example 1.6.1

Among elementary school teachers, those who are teaching in year-round schools will report having higher morale than those who are teaching in elementary schools that follow a more traditional school-year schedule.

Improved Version of Example 1.6.1

Elementary school teachers who teach in year-round schools have higher morale than those who teach on a traditional schedule.

➤ Guideline 1.7 A hypothesis should indicate what will actually be studied—not the possible implications of a study or value judgments of the author.

Because the hypothesis in Example 1.7.1 cannot be tested within a reasonable time frame, it is most likely a statement of implications. The improved version probably reflects more accurately the methodology that the author plans to use. If the hypothesis is supported by data, the author may choose to speculate in the discussion section of the research report that in the future, baby boomers will become more like the currently retired population in their attitudes on social issues.

Example 1.7.1

The liberalization of Americans' attitudes on social issues will take a dramatic turn when baby boomers reach retirement age.

Improved Version of Example 1.7.1

Retired Americans have more conservative attitudes on social issues than baby boomers.

In Example 1.7.2, the author is expressing a value judgment rather than the anticipated relationship between the variables to be studied. The improved version indicates how "religion" will be treated as a variable (i.e., attendance at religious services) and indicates the specific outcome (i.e., cheating behavior) that will be studied.

Example 1.7.2

Religion is good for society.

Improved Version of Example 1.7.2

Attendance at religious services is inversely associated with students' cheating behavior while taking classroom tests.

Note that if the hypothesis in the Improved Version of Example 1.7.2 is supported by data, the researcher may want to assert that less cheating is "good for society" in his or her research report. Such an assertion is acceptable as long as the researcher makes it clear that the assertion is a value judgment and not a data-based conclusion.

➢ Guideline 1.8   A hypothesis usually should name variables in the order in which they occur or will be measured.

In Example 1.8.1, the natural order has been reversed because the deprivation will precede, and possibly produce, the anticipated anxiety. This problem has been corrected in the improved version.

Example 1.8.1

More free-floating anxiety will be observed among adults who are subjected to longer periods of sensory deprivation.

Improved Version of Example 1.8.1

Adults who are subjected to extended periods of sensory deprivation will experience more free-floating anxiety than those exposed to less deprivation.

In Example 1.8.2, the natural order has been reversed. Because College Boards are almost always taken prior to entering college, they should be mentioned before freshman grades. The problem has been corrected in the improved version.

Example 1.8.2
There is a positive relationship between first-semester grades earned in college and College Board Scholastic Aptitude Test scores.

Improved Version of Example 1.8.2
There is a positive relationship between College Board Scholastic Aptitude Test scores and grades earned in college.

➢ Guideline 1.9 Avoid using the words "significant" or "significance" in a hypothesis.

The terms "significant" and "significance" usually refer to tests of statistical significance. Because most empirical studies include these tests, reference to them in hypotheses is not necessary; sophisticated readers will assume that the issue of statistical significance will be dealt with in the results section of the research report.

➢ Guideline 1.10 Avoid using the word "prove" in a hypothesis.

Empirical research relies on observations or measurements that are less than perfectly reliable; they usually involve only samples from populations. In addition, there may be biases in procedures. For these reasons, errors are almost always present in the results of empirical studies. Thus, we do not claim to *prove* something with empirical research methods. Instead, we gather data that offer varying degrees of confidence regarding various conclusions.

➢ Guideline 1.11   Avoid using two different terms to refer to the same variable in a hypothesis.

In Example 1.11.1, it is not clear whether the "literature-based approach" is the same as the "new approach" since two different terms are being used. This problem has been corrected in the improved version.

Example 1.11.1

Students who receive a literature-based approach to reading instruction plus training in phonetics will have better attitudes toward reading than those who receive only the new approach to reading instruction.

Improved Version of Example 1.11.1

Students who receive a literature-based approach to reading instruction plus training in phonetics will have better attitudes toward reading than those who receive only the literature-based approach to reading instruction.

➢ Guideline 1.12   Avoid making precise statistical predictions in a hypothesis.

Precise statistical predictions are rarely justified. In addition, they may make it almost impossible to confirm a hypothesis. Consider Example 1.12.1. If contamination were reduced by any percentage other than 35, the hypothesis would have to be rejected. For example, if there were a 99% reduction in bacterial contamination, the hypothesis would need to be rejected. Likewise, if there were a 1% reduction, the hypothesis would need to be rejected. The improved version indicates the direction of the relationship without naming a precise statistical outcome.

Example 1.12.1

Thirty-five percent less bacterial contamination will be found in the air of operating rooms in which the staff wears polypropylene coveralls than in the air of operating rooms in which they wear conventional surgical clothing.

Improved Version of Example 1.12.1

Less bacterial contamination will be found in the air of operating rooms in which the staff wears polypropylene coveralls than in the air of operating rooms in which they wear conventional surgical clothing.

Exercise for Chapter 1

The following questions are provided for review and classroom discussion. Because the application of many of the guidelines involves a certain amount of subjectivity, there may be some legitimate differences of opinions on the best answers to some of the questions.

PART A: Name the two variables in each of the following hypotheses.

1. Middle socioeconomic status (SES) students participate in more extracurricular activities than do low SES students.

2. Among college graduates, authoritarianism and anxiety are directly related.

3. Homeless women are subjected to more sexual abuse than are housed women.

4. Children who are shown a film with numerous instances of physical violence will demonstrate more aggressiveness during a free play period than children who are shown a control film without violence.

5. Among first graders, there is a direct relationship between level of eye-hand coordination and achievement in mathematics.

PART B: For each of the following hypotheses, name the guideline(s), if any, that were not followed. Revise each hypothesis that you think is faulty. In your revisions, you may need to make some assumptions about what the authors had in mind when writing the hypotheses.

6. The hypothesis is to prove that first-born boys are more athletically competitive than are second-born boys.

7. Children differ in age, and they also differ in their ability to attend to instructional presentations.

8. The rate of development of speech in young children is directly related to the verbal fluency of their parents.

9. Among high achievers, there will be a higher level of sibling rivalry.

10. Other things being equal, more rewards result in better performance.

11. The social agenda of the present administration is weak.

12. There is a direct relationship between a mechanical engineer's ability to visualize objects rotating in space and his success on the job.

13. There will be less test-taking anxiety among college applicants who take a test-preparation course.

14. The reading achievement of first-graders whose parents read to them on a regular basis will be significantly greater.

15. Students who take Psychology 101 will report greater self-insight than students who do not take introductory psychology.

16. Various subcultures view the school environment differently.

17. People who cheat the welfare system are disreputable.

18. The use of condoms by adolescents who take the ABC AIDS Awareness Course will be 73% greater than that of the control group.

PART C: Write a simple hypothesis on a topic of interest to you. Include in the hypothesis a reference to a population. Underline the names of the two variables.

Chapter 2

A Closer Look at Hypotheses

This chapter presents some advanced guidelines for writing hypotheses and explores some of the principles from Chapter 1 in greater detail.

> **Guideline 2.1   A "statement of the hypothesis" may contain more than one hypothesis. It is permissible to include them in a single sentence as long as the sentence is reasonably concise and its meaning is clear.**

In Example 2.1.1, there is one independent variable (supplementary group therapy) and two anticipated outcomes or dependent variables. Therefore, there are two hypotheses: (1) those who receive the group therapy supplement will report more relief, and (2) those who receive the group therapy supplement will be more satisfied with the counseling process.

Example 2.1.1

Clients experiencing mild levels of depression will report more relief from their symptoms and greater satisfaction with the counseling process when individual therapy is supplemented with group therapy.

Note that in Example 2.1.1, the reader must infer that there probably will be a comparison or control group that will not receive group therapy because the comparisons that begin with "more" and "greater" have not been completed. This violation of Guideline 1.4 in Chapter 1 is sometimes found in published research reports. However, it would be desirable to end the hypothesis with "than clients who receive only individual therapy."

➤ Guideline 2.2 When a number of related hypotheses are to be stated, consider presenting them in a numbered or lettered list.

Example 2.2.1 shows four of the 14 related hypotheses stated by researchers for a study of male/female differences in adolescent sexuality.

Example 2.2.1

It was hypothesized that females will:
1. be less likely to engage in premarital sexual intercourse.
2. be more committed to sexual abstinence.
3. be less permissive in their sexual attitudes.
4. see having premarital adolescent sex as a greater impediment to achieving future life goals.[1]

➤ Guideline 2.3 The hypothesis or hypotheses should be placed before the section on methods.

The method section of a research report describes how the researcher tested the hypothesis. Therefore, the hypothesis should be stated before describing the methods used.

In journal articles, hypotheses are usually stated in the paragraph immediately preceding the major heading of "Method." In theses and dissertations, the placement is usually the same, although there may be some variations depending on the style manual in use at a particular institution.

➤ Guideline 2.4 It is permissible to use terms other than the term "hypothesis" to refer to a hypothesis.

The context and placement of the statement just before the method section usually make it clear that a hypothesis is being stated. In Example 2.4.1, the researcher describes her *expectation*, which is her hypothesis.

---

[1] De Gaston, Weed, & Jensen (1996, pp. 224-225).

Example 2.4.1

It was expected that American women would be more likely than American men to believe that there is gender-based wage disparity.[2]

Other writers begin the statements of their hypotheses with phrases such as "In light of the literature review, it was predicted that…" and "We speculated that.…" Generally, however, it is better to use the formal term "hypothesis" or one of its derivatives in phrases such as "In light of the literature review, it was hypothesized that…" or "The hypothesis is that.…"

Note that in a research proposal, the present tense should be used (e.g., "The hypothesis is…") while in a research report, the past tense is usually more appropriate (e.g., "The hypothesis was…").

➢ Guideline 2.5   In a research report, a hypothesis should flow from the narrative that immediately precedes it.

A research report typically begins with an introduction and literature review, which we will consider in detail in a later chapter. These elements of a report should logically lead the reader to the hypothesis. Example 2.5.1 is the last paragraph in a combined introduction and literature review. As you can see, the last sentence in the paragraph flows directly from the preceding material.

Example 2.5.1

These findings [presented in the literature review above] suggest that AIDS prevention programs for youth at risk of HIV infection are likely to yield short-term changes in attitudes and behaviors. It is not clear, however, if such changes can be maintained over time. Therefore, it is important to follow troubled youth who received an AIDS prevention intervention over longer periods. This study examined whether cognitive/behavioral interventions that produced immediate changes in AIDS-related knowledge, attitudes, and intentions among delinquents and abused adolescents (Auslander, et al., 1992) are capable of producing long-term benefits assessed at the 9- to 12-month follow-up. Specifically, it was hypothesized that adolescents who participated in an intensive 9-session AIDS prevention program will (a) know more about AIDS, (b) hold more positive

---

[2] Browne (1997, p. 109).

attitudes toward prevention, and (c) report engagement in fewer unsafe activities than would their counterparts in a control group at follow-up.[3]

➢ Guideline 2.6 A hypothesis may be stated without indicating the type of relationship expected between variables. To qualify as a hypothesis, however, it must specify that some unknown type of relationship is expected.

A hypothesis that states that an unknown type of relationship exists is called a *nondirectional hypothesis*. (Up to this point in this book, all of the hypotheses have been *directional*.) Example 2.6.1 illustrates a *nondirectional hypothesis* for a nonexperimental study. Notice that the hypothesis does *not* indicate which group of police officers is predicted to be higher in their level of authoritarianism; it just states that the two groups differ.

Example 2.6.1

Police officers who were reared in low socioeconomic status families differ in their level of authoritarianism from police officers who were reared in middle socioeconomic status families.

Example 2.6.2 shows a nondirectional hypothesis for an experimental study.

Example 2.6.2

Adult males with condition X who are administered Drug A will report a different level of pain than a comparable group of adult males who receive Drug B.

Nondirectional hypotheses are less frequently used in research than directional hypotheses. This is probably true for two reasons: (1) researchers often have opinions about the variables they study, and their opinions usually lead them to formulate directional hypotheses, and (2) when researchers do not want to speculate on the direction of a relationship, they may use a statement of the research purpose or a

---

[3] Slonim-Nevo, Auslander, Ozawa, & Jung (1996, p. 411).

research question instead of a hypothesis. This type of substitution is discussed in detail in Chapter 3.

➢ Guideline 2.7   When a researcher has a research hypothesis, it should be stated in the research report; the null hypothesis need not always be stated.

A *research hypothesis* is the hypothesis that a researcher believes will be supported by his or her data. The *null hypothesis* is a *statistical hypothesis* that states that any difference is attributable to random errors; in other words, it says that there is no true difference—only a random one. Significance tests are used to test the null hypothesis. (Those of you who have not taken a statistics course should consult Appendix C for an introduction to the null hypothesis and significance testing.)

In journal articles, formal statements of null hypotheses are almost always omitted since they always have the same content—regardless of how they are worded, they always attribute any differences to random errors. Thus, it would be redundant to state the null hypothesis in journal article after journal article.

In term projects, theses, and dissertations, however, students are often required to state null hypotheses in order to demonstrate that they understand the purpose of the significance tests they conducted. Examples 2.7.1 and 2.7.2 illustrate some ways the null hypothesis can be stated. Because there is more than one way to word a null hypothesis, two statements are shown in each example. Only one statement, however, should be used in a research report.

Example 2.7.1

RESEARCH HYPOTHESIS:

Social standing in campus organizations is directly related to gregariousness.

ONE VERSION OF THE CORRESPONDING NULL HYPOTHESIS:

There is no true relationship between social standing in campus organizations and gregariousness.

ANOTHER VERSION OF THE CORRESPONDING NULL HYPOTHESIS:

The relationship between social standing in campus organizations and gregariousness is nonexistent in the population from which the sample was drawn.

Example 2.7.2

RESEARCH HYPOTHESIS:

Private school graduates have a higher proportion of fathers in high status occupations than public school graduates.

ONE VERSION OF THE CORRESPONDING NULL HYPOTHESIS:

There is no true difference in the proportion of fathers in high status occupations between the populations of private school and public school graduates.

ANOTHER VERSION OF THE CORRESPONDING NULL HYPOTHESIS:

The observed difference between the proportions of fathers in high status occupations for private school graduates and public school graduates is the result of chance variations associated with the random sampling process.

Exercise for Chapter 2

In this exercise, you are asked to review examples of published research in journals as well as theses and dissertations. There is no better way to learn the conventions followed in writing reports of empirical research than by extensive reading of such reports. Keep in mind that statements of the hypotheses are usually placed just above the heading "Method" in research reports.

1. Review journal articles and locate a statement that contains two or more hypotheses incorporated into a single sentence. Copy the statement and bring it to class for discussion.

2. Review journal articles and locate a statement that consists of a numbered or lettered list of three or more hypotheses. Copy the list and bring it to class for discussion.

3. Review four journal articles that contain explicit statements of hypotheses and make note of the following:

   a. In how many cases are the hypotheses stated in the last paragraph before the heading "Method"?

   b. In how many cases are the hypotheses stated in the last sentence before the heading "Method"?

   c. In how many cases did the authors use alternative terms such as "predict" or "expect" instead of "hypothesize" in the statements of the hypotheses?

   d. How many of the hypotheses are directional, and how many are nondirectional? If both types are found, copy an example of each.

4. Examine theses or dissertations in your college/university library. Do any of them contain statements of the null hypothesis? If yes, copy one and bring it to class for discussion.

5. Write a directional research hypothesis on a topic of interest to you. Then write a corresponding null hypothesis for it.

6. Rewrite the directional hypothesis that you wrote for question 5 to make it nondirectional.

Notes:

Chapter 3

Writing Research Purposes, Objectives, and Questions

Often researchers do not state hypotheses either because they are not interested in examining relationships between variables or because they believe that there is too little knowledge on a topic to permit formulation of hypotheses. Under these circumstances, a *research purpose* (also called a *research objective*) or a *research question* should be substituted for a hypothesis.

The principles for writing hypotheses should be followed when writing research purposes and questions. The following principles indicate when to state the latter instead of hypotheses and illustrate the application of some of the principles in Chapters 1 and 2 when writing purposes and questions.

➢ Guideline 3.1 When the goal of research is to describe group(s) without describing relationships among variables, write a research purpose or question instead of a hypothesis.

As you recall from Chapter 1, a simple research hypothesis predicts a relationship between two variables. Note that in Example 3.1.1, no relationships are being examined; the researchers want to determine only one thing—the level of public support. Hence it would be inappropriate to try to state it as a hypothesis. A statement of the purpose is appropriate.

Example 3.1.1

Our purpose was to determine the level of public support for the bond issue for funding the construction of additional public libraries.

Likewise, no relationship is implied in Example 3.1.2. Instead, the researchers want to determine only what is being done to provide ethical training.

Example 3.1.2

The purpose of our research was to determine what traditional graduate training programs in nursing were doing to provide practical training on ethical issues regarding euthanasia.

Notice that Examples 3.1.1 and 3.1.2 could have been stated as research questions, as illustrated in Example 3.1.3.

Example 3.1.3

What is the level of public support for the bond issue for funding the construction of additional public libraries?

What are traditional graduate training programs in nursing doing to provide practical training on ethical issues regarding euthanasia?

The choice between stating a research purpose or a research question is a matter of choosing the form that reads more smoothly in a particular context. One form is not inherently preferable to the other.

➢ Guideline 3.2   When there is insufficient evidence to permit formulation of a hypothesis regarding a relationship between variables, write a research purpose or question.

The researchers who wrote Example 3.2.1 note in their literature review that there have been no previous studies on the possible relationship between how married women feel about themselves and whether they change their names when they marry. In light of this lack of previous research, they stated a question instead of a hypothesis.

Example 3.2.1

Research Question: Do women who adopt their husbands' surnames differ in their level of self-esteem from those who retain their surnames or combine their surnames with their husbands' surnames?[1]

---

[1] Paraphrased from Stafford & Kline (1996, p. 85).

20

Example 3.2.1 could be rewritten as a research purpose without changing the meaning of the authors' statement, as illustrated in Example 3.2.2.

Example 3.2.2

Research Purpose: To determine whether women who adopt their husband's surnames differ in their level of self-esteem from those who retain their surnames or combine their surnames with their husbands' surnames.

➢ Guideline 3.3   The research purpose or question should be as specific as possible, yet stated concisely.

The need for specificity in hypotheses is discussed in Chapters 1 and 2. Application of this guideline to hypotheses, purposes, and questions is often more problematic than one might realize at first. Consider, for instance, Example 3.3.1. It is quite specific, actually naming two specific scales (i.e., measuring tools). However, for readers who are not familiar with the specific instruments, the research purpose may be too specific.[2] Thus, writers must judge whether their audiences are likely to be familiar with the specific item(s) mentioned—in this case, the specific scales.

Example 3.3.1

The purpose was to determine whether scores on the HIV Knowledge and Attitudes Scales are correlated with scores on the Johnson Job Stress Scale among laboratory technicians who handle blood specimens obtained from patients who may be HIV+.

For readers who are not familiar with the specific scales, the Improved Version of Example 3.3.1 is superior.

Improved Version of Example 3.3.1

The purpose was to determine whether knowledge of and attitudes toward HIV are correlated with self-reported job stress among laboratory technicians who handle blood specimens obtained from patients who may be HIV+.

---

[2] Instruments such as attitude scales need to be described in detail in the section of the research report on methods. This topic is covered in Chapter 8.

➤ Guideline 3.4   When a number of related purposes or questions are to be stated, consider presenting them in a numbered or lettered list.

In Example 3.4.1, the researchers present numbered questions.

Example 3.4.1

In sum, the following questions guided our study: (1) How important do teachers perceive the six aspects of student motivation for reading in the classroom [described in the literature review]? (2) How are teacher perceptions of student motivation related to reading achievement? (3) To what extent do teacher perceptions of student reading motivation vary across grade levels?[3]

The numbered list in Example 3.4.1 allows the researcher to refer to individual hypotheses by number later in the research report; this possibility is discussed in Chapter 9.

➤ Guideline 3.5   In a research report, a research purpose or question should flow from the narrative that immediately precedes it.

A research report typically begins with an introduction and literature review. These elements of a report should logically lead the reader to the research purpose or question. Example 3.5.1 is drawn from the last paragraph in an introduction that included a literature review. In the first sentence of the example, the authors make a transition that leads to the purpose of the study.

Example 3.5.1

It is clear from this brief review [of literature presented above] that educational and cultural differences between Western and Asian societies are likely to result in differences in the self-regulated learning behavior of students in these societies. The purpose of this study was to identify some of these differences by comparing the strategy use of groups of students whose educational experiences were culturally diverse.[4]

---

[3] Sweet, Guthrie, & Ng (1998, p. 213).
[4] Purdie & Hattie (1996, p. 849).

Exercise for Chapter 3

1. Name the two conditions under which it would be better to state a research purpose or question rather than a research hypothesis.

2. In general, should the research question format be preferred over the research purpose format?

3. Review journal articles and locate a statement that consists of a numbered list of research purposes or questions. Copy the list and bring it to class for discussion.

4. Review four journal articles that contain statements of purposes or questions and make note of the following:

   a. In how many cases are the purposes or questions presented in the last paragraph before the section on methods?

   b. In how many cases are the purposes or questions stated in the last sentence before the section on methods?

5. Write a research purpose on a topic of interest to you. Then rewrite it as a research question. Which form (i.e., purpose or question) do you prefer? Why?

Notes:

Chapter 4

Writing Titles

The following are guidelines for writing titles for empirical research reports.

➤ Guideline 4.1 If only a small number of variables are studied, the title should name the variables.

In Example 4.1.1, there are two variables: (1) self-esteem and (2) aggressiveness.

Example 4.1.1
The Relationship Between Self-Esteem and Aggressiveness

Notice that the title in the example is not a complete sentence and does not end with a period mark, which are appropriate characteristics of titles.

➤ Guideline 4.2 If many variables are studied, only the *types* of variables should be named.

Suppose a researcher examined how students' attitudes toward school change over time with attention to differences among urban, suburban, and rural groups; various socioeconomic groups; the sexes; and so on. Because there are too many variables to name in a concise title, only the main variable(s) need to be specifically named; the others may be referred to by type, as was done in Example 4.2.1, where the term "demographic variables" stands for a variety of background variables such as socioeconomic status and gender.

Example 4.2.1

Changes in Students' Attitudes Toward School and Their Relationships with Selected Demographic Variables

➢ Guideline 4.3   The title of a journal article should be concise; the title of a thesis or dissertation may be longer.

Titles of journal articles tend to be concise. A simple survey illustrates this point. A count of the number of words in the titles of a random sample of 152 research articles on mathematics education that appeared in 42 journals in a recent year revealed that the median (average) number of words was close to 11. Example 4.3.1 is the shortest one identified in the survey; it is exceptionally short and could be improved by incorporating reference to the variables studied.

Example 4.3.1

The Mathematics Department

Example 4.3.2 is the longest one identified in the survey. It is long only because the specific countries are listed. If it ended with "in Various Countries" instead of the list, it would be more concise but less descriptive.

Example 4.3.2

Grade Placement of Addition and Subtraction Topics in Japan, Mainland China, the Soviet Union, Taiwan, and the United States

Example 4.3.3 shows a title of about average length for the sample of titles examined. It illustrates Guideline 4.2; the *types* of variables, "personality factors" and "biographical factors," are referred to; the specific personality traits and types of biographical data collected are not spelled out.

Example 4.3.3

Contributions of Some Personality and Biographical Factors to Mathematical Creativity

For a random sample of titles of dissertations on mathematics education during the same recent year, the average number of words in the titles was almost 19, which is considerably more than the average of 11 for journal articles. The longest dissertation title is shown in Example 4.3.4.

Example 4.3.4

A Descriptive Study of Verbal Problems in Mathematics Textbooks Grades Seven and Eight, from Five Time Periods: The Early 60s, the Early 70s, the Late 70s, the Early 80s, and the Late 80s

Ask your instructor or chair of your thesis or dissertation committee whether they want you to write a concise title, such as those commonly used in journals, or a longer title, which is more typical (but not universal) in theses and dissertations.

➤ Guideline 4.4   A title should indicate what was studied —not the results or conclusions of the study.

All the previous examples illustrate this principle. Example 4.4.1 violates the principle; it is corrected in the improved version.

Example 4.4.1

Work-Based Learning Negatively Affects Some Aspects of School Performance Such as Having Time for Homework

Improved Version of Example 4.4.1

Work-Based Learning: Student Perspectives on Quality and Links to School[1]

Guideline 4.4 may surprise some beginning students of empirical methods because results and conclusions are often stated in titles in the popular press. This is the case because the press often reports straightforward facts; "Five Die in Downtown Hotel Fire" is a perfectly acceptable title for a factual article of limited scope. Because empirical research reports are likely to raise as many questions as they resolve, a title that states a simple factual result or conclusion is usually inappropriate.

---

[1] Stasz, C. & Brewer, D. J. (1998, p. 31).

➢ Guideline 4.5   Mention the population(s) in a title when the type(s) of populations are important.

In Example 4.5.1, the population consists of teachers. This is important because the reactions of parents or students might be quite different from those of teachers.

Example 4.5.1

Teachers' Reactions to the Use of Calculators by Primary Level Students During Mathematics Examinations

➢ Guideline 4.6   Consider the use of subtitles to amplify the purposes or methods of study.

In Examples 4.6.1 and 4.6.2, the subtitles indicate the research methods used. In Example 4.6.3, the subtitle suggests a purpose: to compare two types of counselors.

Example 4.6.1

The Role of Alcoholism in Dysfunctional Families: A Qualitative Study

Example 4.6.2

Kindergarten Teachers' Definitions of Literacy: A National Survey

Example 4.6.3

Counseling Clients with Traumatic Stress Syndrome: Perspectives of Experienced and Novice Counselors

➢ Guideline 4.7   A title may be in the form of a question; this form should be used sparingly and with caution.

Example 4.7.1 implies that the result will be a simple "yes" or "no" answer, which is seldom the case in empirical research. Remember that empirical methods give us only varying degrees of confidence in results—not final answers. In the First Improved Version of Example 4.7.1, the problem has been fixed by posing the question in such a way that it cannot be answered with a simple "yes" or "no." The Second Improved Version of Example 4.7.1 shows that the problem can be avoided by not using the question form.

Example 4.7.1

Do Private Colleges and Universities Provide Access to Physically Handicapped Students?

First Improved Version of Example 4.7.1

To What Extent Do Private Colleges and Universities Provide Access to Physically Handicapped Students?

Second Improved Version of Example 4.7.1

Access for Physically Disabled Students at Private Colleges and Universities

Questions, when used as titles, have a less formal feel than titles in the form of statements. Thus, the question form sometimes is preferred in less formal types of publications such as staff newsletters and workshop materials.

➢ Guideline 4.8   In titles, use the words "effect" and "influence" with caution.

The words "effect" and influence" are frequently used in the titles of research reports in which cause-and-effect relationships are studied. To examine such relationships, true experimental, quasi-experimental, or rigorous ex post facto methods should be employed. As a general rule, only reports on these methods should contain these words in their titles.

Examples 4.8.1 and 4.8.2 illustrate the typical use of the word "effect" in a title. The general form is: "The effects of an independent variable (treatments or stimulus) on a dependent variable (outcome or response)."

Example 4.8.1

The Effects of Three Schedules of Reinforcement on the Maze Performance of Rats

Example 4.8.2

Effects of Wellness, Fitness, and Sport-Skills Programs on Body Image and Lifestyle Behaviors[2]

Note that "effect" is used as a noun in the two examples. As a noun, it means "influence." When used as a noun, the word "affect" means "feelings or emotions." Clearly, "effect" is the correct noun to use in these examples.

➢ Guideline 4.9   A title should be consistent with the research hypothesis, purpose, or question.

In Example 4.9.1, a research purpose is stated. The corresponding title closely mirrors the statement of the purpose.

Example 4.9.1

RESEARCH HYPOTHESIS: The major purpose in doing this study, therefore, was to determine how practicing teachers acquired their understanding of cooperative learning and what that understanding looked like in classrooms, particularly middle level (i.e., grades 5–9) classrooms.

CORRESPONDING TITLE: Cooperative Learning: An Investigation of the Knowledge and Classroom Practice of Middle Grade Teachers[3]

In Example 4.9.2, the title refers to the variable named in the hypothesis.

Example 4.9.2

RESEARCH HYPOTHESIS: We hypothesized that clerks may sell cigarettes significantly more often to Black children than to their White counterparts who are matched for age, sex, and behavior.

CORRESPONDING TITLE: Racial Discrimination in Minors' Access to Tobacco[4]

---

[2] Koff & Bauman, (1997, p. 555).
[3] Sparapani, Abel, Easton, Edwards, & Herbster (1997, p. 251–252).
[4] Landrine, Klonoff, & Alcaraz (1997, p. 135).

30

➢ Guideline 4.10   Consider mentioning unique features of a study in its title.

Suppose you conducted the first long-term follow-up study on the effects of a drug. You would be wise to indicate that your study is a long-term one in the title, as shown in example 4.10.1.

Example 4.10.1
The Long-Term Effects of Tetracycline on Tooth Enamel Erosion

➢ Guideline 4.11   Avoid clever titles, especially if they fail to communicate important information about the report.

In Example 4.11.1, only "Publishing Criminal Justice Research" is informative. The reader will assume that an article deals with contemporary issues unless the title indicates that the study is historical; thus, reference to the new millennium is not needed. The subtitle is completely uninformative. It vaguely refers to what is *not* covered—instead, it should specifically indicate what *is* presented in the report.

Example 4.11.1
Publishing Criminal Justice Research in the New Millennium: Things Gutenberg Never Taught You

In general, throughout research reports, avoid the temptation to be clever or humorous. The function of a research report is to inform—not entertain.

Exercise for Chapter 4

PART A: Comment on the adequacy of each of the following titles for research articles.

1. Registered Nurses Have Less Unfounded Fear of HIV Infection Than Nursing Assistants

2. Watering the Proverbial Garden: Factors Affecting Effective Communication Between Teachers and School Administrators

3. The Clinical Psychologist

4. Are Age and Tenure Related to the Job Satisfaction of Social Workers?

5. Can Psychotherapists Prevent Suicide?

6. The Effects of Massive and Moderate Levels of Verbal Praise on Out-of-Seat Behavior of Hyperactive Students

7. The Effects of Peer Coaching in Reading Among Fifth Graders: An Experiment Conducted in Five Major Urban Areas During the 1998-1999 School Year Using Multiple Measures of Reading Comprehension with Analyses by Gender and Grade Level

8. Forbidden Fruit Tastes Especially Sweet: A Study of Lawyers' Ethical Behavior

9. Do Students Retain More Mathematical Concepts When They Learn Them Using Hands-on Instruction?

PART B: Select two of the hypotheses, purposes, or questions presented in Chapters 1, 2, or 3, and write an appropriate title for each.

PART C: Name a purpose for research on a topic of interest to you, and write an appropriate title.

Chapter 5

Writing Introductions and Literature Reviews

The purpose of an introduction in an empirical research report is to introduce the problem area, establish its importance, and indicate the author's perspectives on the problem. Introductions usually conclude with an explicit statement of the research hypotheses, purposes, or questions to be explored in the study.

In a journal article, the introduction is almost always integrated with the literature review into a single essay. In theses and dissertations, it is common to have the first chapter present the introduction and the second one present the literature review.

The guidelines that follow apply to all types of empirical research reports and proposals, except where noted.

➢ Guideline 5.1 Start the introduction by describing the problem area; gradually shift its focus to specific research hypotheses, purposes, or questions.

To implement the first guideline, write a topic outline of what will be covered. Example 5.1.1 shows a simple outline that starts with the broad topic and becomes more specific, ending with research purposes.

Example 5.1.1

Topic Outline for the Introduction

1. Importance of question-asking by children
   a. As a skill used in learning in school
   b. As a functional skill in the home and other nonschool settings
2. Introduction to two types of questions
   a. Request for factual information (who, what, and when)
   b. Questions about causation (why)
   c. Functions of the two types in school

3. Relationship between parents' and children's verbal behavior
    a. On other verbal variables
    b. On question-asking behavior: quantity and type
4. Relationship between culture and verbal behavior
    a. Examples of how and why cultures may vary in their question-asking behavior
    b. Functions of questions in target cultures
5. Statement of the research purposes
    a. Determine types and numbers of questions asked by children in a structured learning environment
    b. Determine the relationship between question-asking by children and by parents, with attention to both number and type
    c. Determine differences in question-asking behavior among target cultures

If this outline were for a thesis or dissertation, the author would write the introduction with an emphasis on his or her own views and observations regarding these topics with few citations of published literature. It would be appropriate to point out that the topics will be covered in more detail in the literature review, which is usually the second chapter.

If Example 5.1.1 were an outline for an introduction to a journal article, the literature review would be integrated with the author's introductory remarks.

➢ Guideline 5.2   Start long introductions and literature reviews with a paragraph that describes their organization, and use subheadings to guide readers.

The numbered topics in Example 5.1.1 (e.g., *Importance of question-asking by children* and *Introduction to two types of questions*) could be used as subheadings.

In theses and dissertations, where the introduction and literature review are usually each a fairly long chapter, the use of subheadings is especially desirable. Begin each chapter with an overview of what is covered in it, and begin each subsection with such an overview. This is illustrated in Example 5.2.1 in which the first paragraph provides an overview of the chapter, and the second paragraph provides an overview of the first subsection.

Example 5.2.1

CHAPTER 2

LITERATURE REVIEW

This chapter describes literature relevant to the research purposes of this thesis. It is organized into four sections: (1) the importance of question-asking by children, (2) an introduction to two basic types of questions, (3) the relationship between parents' and children's verbal behavior, and (4) the relationship between culture and verbal behavior. At the end of each section, the relevance of the literature to the research reported in this thesis is discussed.

Importance of Question-Asking by Children

Most of the literature on the importance of question-asking deals with the behavior of students in school settings during learning activities. This literature is reviewed first in order to establish the importance of question-asking as a tool in the learning/teaching process. Then, the more limited literature on question-asking by children as a functional skill in the home and other nonschool settings is reviewed. Throughout, there is an emphasis on the principles of learning theories as well as theories of social interaction that underlie the literature.

Two major studies examined the relationship between students' question-asking behavior and. . . .

➢ Guideline 5.3   The importance of a topic should be explicitly stated in the introduction to a term paper, thesis, or dissertation.

Colleges and universities often require that the introduction to a thesis or dissertation contain a subsection on the importance of the research topic.[1] Be specific in giving reasons for the importance of the topic, as illustrated in Example 5.3.1.

Example 5.3.1

The need to investigate the training needs of counselors who work with persons with AIDS is important because (1) AIDS continues to be a public health crisis; (2) AIDS tends to occur more frequently in certain minority groups, which may have unique psychological needs; and (3) information on the disease and its treatment continues to emerge at a rapid rate, creating the need for ongoing training of counselors.

---

[1] This subsection often has the heading, "Significance of the Problem." To avoid confusion with the issue of statistical significance, we suggest the headings "Practical Significance of the Problem" or "Importance of the Problem."

35

Long, detailed statements on the importance of research topics are less common, although usually acceptable, in journal articles. Authors of articles often assume that their readers are specialists who already understand the importance of the topics. Thus, they often provide less detailed statements than are typically found in theses and dissertations. It is always a good idea, however, to indicate at least briefly why the topic of the research is important.

➤ Guideline 5.4   A statement on the importance of a topic should be specific to the topic investigated.

Example 5.4.1 was submitted as the statement on the importance of a topic in the first draft of a proposal for a thesis in which a functional skills program in adult schools was to be evaluated. Notice that the statement fails to deal specifically with functional skills in adult education. In fact, the statement is so broad that it could refer to almost any curriculum and instruction topic in education, which is clearly a violation of the guideline.

Example 5.4.1

Human resource is one of the greatest resources of this country, and education plays a major role in maintaining, nurturing, and protecting that resource. Thus, it is imperative that we find, evaluate, and utilize educational systems that yield the results necessary for the country's progress.

➤ Guideline 5.5   Use of the first person is acceptable; it should be used when it facilitates the smooth flow of the introduction.

Use of the first person is especially appropriate when referring to the author's personal observations, experiences, and beliefs, as is the case in Example 5.5.1. The use of "I" in this example is less stilted than using the term "the author" to refer to the writer.

Example 5.5.1

I began to speculate on the origins of this problem during my three years as an assistant to a teacher of the learning disabled.

Frequent use of the first person throughout the introduction and elsewhere in a research report, however, can be distracting. In Example 5.5.2, the first person is overused.

Example 5.5.2

When I realized that all the previous research on this topic was nonexperimental, I decided that I would undertake an experimental study.

Improved Version of Example 5.5.2

Because all the previous research on this topic was nonexperimental, an experimental study seemed desirable.

➢ Guideline 5.6   The literature review should be presented in the form of an essay—not in the form of an annotated list.

An annotation is a brief summary of contents; a list of annotations indicates what research is available on a topic but fails to organize the material for the reader by indicating how the individual citations relate to one another and what trends the researcher has observed in the published literature on his or her topic.

An effective review of literature is an essay organized around a topic outline (see Guideline 5.1) that takes the reader from topic to topic. The literature on a topic is cited during a discussion of that topic. Research reports with similar findings or methodologies may be cited together, as in Example 5.6.1 where several references are cited for each of the two findings mentioned.

Example 5.6.1

Inadequate social support has been associated with less optimal birth outcomes, including the delivery of low birthweight infants (Norbeck & Anderson, 1989; Seguin, Potvin, St. Denis, & Loiselle, 1995). Other studies have documented poor birth outcomes following prenatal depression (Steer, Scholl, Hediger, & Fisher, 1992; Wadhwa, Sandan, Parto, Dunkel-Schetter, & Garite, 1993). Steer and colleagues found that severely depressed women were three times more likely to deliver babies that were low birthweight, preterm, or small-for-gestational age.[2]

---

[2] Cook, Selig, Wedge, & Gohn-Baube (1999, p. 130).

Example 5.6.2 also illustrates this guideline. Notice that the excerpt is organized around topics—not the findings of individual researchers. In fact, three of the references are each cited two times—in support of different contentions.

Example 5.6.2

There is now substantial evidence that it is those who say they drink to cope with, or escape from, unpleasant or stressful situations or emotions who are most likely to be problem drinkers (Abbey, Smith, & Scott, 1993; Cooper, Russell, & George, 1988; Farer, Khavan, & Douglass, 1980; Neff, 1997; M. J. Smith, Abbey, & Scott, 1993). Whereas drinking to escape tends to be viewed as problematic or pathological, drinking for social or enjoyment reasons is not...associated with increased alcohol consumption and frequent heavy drinking (M. J. Smith et al., 1993). Indeed, it seems that alcohol consumption, even at high levels, is more likely to translate into problem drinking for individuals who strongly endorse escapist reasons for drinking than for those who give social reasons for drinking (Abbey et al., 1993; Cooper et al., 1988).[3]

Note that in the Harvard method for citing references, only the authors' last names and year of publication are given. The names may be made part of the sentence, as in Example 5.6.3, or they may be included parenthetically, as in Example 5.6.4. In Example 5.6.3, the emphasis is on the authorship; in Example 5.6.4, the emphasis is on the content or idea being expressed. The choice of forms depends on the desired emphasis.

Example 5.6.3

Doe (1992) reported that a major source of dissatisfaction among teachers appears to be the low social status accorded their profession.

Example 5.6.4

A major source of dissatisfaction among teachers appears to be the low social status accorded their profession (Doe, 1992).

➤ Guideline 5.7   The literature review should emphasize the findings of previous research—not just the research methodologies and names of variables studied.

---

[3] Grunberg, Moore, Anderson-Connolly, & Greenberg (1999, p. 30).

Example 5.7.1 violates this guideline. In the improved version, the major finding is summarized.

Example 5.7.1

Smith (1998) studied the social dynamics of this group in an intensive two-year case study.

Improved Version of Example 5.7.1

Smith (1998) found that respect for authority among this group declined significantly after the imposition of censorship. Smith's study is important because, being based on a two-year case study, it is the most intensive study to date of the effects of censorship on college students.

➢ Guideline 5.8 Point out trends and themes in the literature.

After reviewing a considerable amount of literature on the social influences on the process of establishing equality in marriages, the authors of Example 5.8.1 pause to make some generalizations about the literature.

Example 5.8.1

As the above literature review suggests, the social context both supports and inhibits the development of marital equality. The factors supporting equality are strong. Today in most families both partners are in the workforce, and men are much more likely to be involved in child care than they were in the past....Yet, the factors that continue to inhibit marital equality are numerous and potent. The power differential between men and women in the larger social context...spills into marriages, often in the form of unexamined gender expectations that reinforce and maintain male power.[4]

➢ Guideline 5.9 Point out gaps in the literature.

In Example 5.9.1, the researchers point out a gap in the literature they reviewed on the determinants of success and failure among college students. Note that the researchers not only point out a gap but also

---

[4] Knudson-Martin & Mahoney (1998, p. 82).

indicate that their study is designed to fill it. This is an effective way to justify a study.

Example 5.9.1

Most theories designed to better understand the determinants of success and failure among college students have focused on social and curricular elements of the immediate college environment (Astin, Tsui, & Avalos, 1996…). Attention to students' family background tends to be limited to consideration of such factors as race and ethnicity, socioeconomic background, and level of parents' or other family members' educational attainment. These studies do not consider characteristics of the students' relationships with their parents or the sorts of parenting practices the students may have experienced during their formative years. The present study addressed this gap. It examined….[5]

In Example 5.9.2, the questions the researchers raise indicate the gaps in the literature on their topic.

Example 5.9.2

Down through the centuries, people have claimed that dreams are invaluable sources for creativity, understanding the unconscious, revealing waking problems, and solving problems (Van de Castle, 1994). Many theories have been developed for how to interpret dreams, but minimal research has been conducted on the effectiveness of dream interpretation. The most research has been done on the recently developed Hill (1996) cognitive-experiential model of dream interpretation. Several studies have found some preliminary evidence that using the Hill method of dream interpretation leads to insight and self-understanding (Cogar & Hill, 1992; Diemer, Lobell, Vivino, & Hill, 1996; Falk & Hill, 1995; Hill, Diemer, Hess, Hillyer, Seeman, 1993). However, many more questions remain to be answered. Are some people more attracted to dream interpretation than others? Is dream interpretation more effective with some volunteer clients than others? What are the most and least helpful components of this dream interpretation model? In the present study, we attempted to address these questions.[6]

Students who are writing term project papers, theses, and dissertations should note that when they point out gaps in the literature, they may be asked by their professors to defend such assertions. Thus, it's a good idea to keep careful records of how the literature search was conducted (i.e., what indices and databases were examined—including the dates) and which descriptors (i.e., subject index terms) were used in the search. Students should consider including a statement such as the one in

---

[5] Strage & Brandt (1999, p. 146).
[6] Hill, Diemer, & Heaton (1997, p. 53).

Example 5.9.3 in their reports; such statements are usually *not* included in journal articles.

Example 5.9.3

A search of the ABC Index for the years 1968 through 2001 using the subject index terms "term a" and "term b" yielded only two surveys (i.e., Doe, 1999; Jones, 2000) and no experimental studies on this topic.

➢ Guideline 5.10   Consider pointing out the number or percentage of people who are affected by the problem you are studying.

Being able to show that many people are affected by a problem may give an author an edge in getting his or her report published. Students who follow this guideline may find that it helps them in getting approval for their proposed topic for a term project, thesis, or dissertation. Of course, the numbers you provide should be specific—not just nonspecific generalizations such as "Many people are…" or "An increasing number of people have…."

The authors of Examples 5.10.1 and 5.10.2 followed this guideline.

Example 5.10.1

During the past quarter century, the number of children ages 18 and under who live in households headed by grandparents has increased by more than 50 percent, from 2.2 million in 1970 to 3.9 million in 1997 (Lugaila, 1998).[7]

Example 5.10.2

From the beginning of the AIDS epidemic through December 1997, the Centers for Disease Control and Prevention reported that 390,692 people in the United States have died of AIDS-related illnesses. AIDS is one of the top three leading causes of death among young women and men aged 25–44 years in the United States (CDC, 1998).[8]

---

[7] Burnette (1999, p. 22).
[8] Ickovics, Druley, Morrill, Grigorenko, & Rodin (1998, p. 958).

➤ Guideline 5.11   Point out how your study differs from previous studies.

Unless you are conducting a strict replication of a previous study, you should point out how your study differs from previously published research. The differences may be in terms of how you conceptualized and measured the variables, the composition of the sample, the method of analysis, and so on. The authors of Example 5.11.1 point out how their study differs from previous ones.

Example 5.11.1

The present study extends previous research by focusing directly on counseling as psychotherapy (as opposed to counseling as tutoring or academic advising) and by investigating the dose–response relationship between amount of counseling and student persistence.[9]

➤ Guideline 5.12   Feel free to express opinions about the quality and importance of the research being cited.

Your reader will assume that the research you are citing is reasonably sound unless you point out otherwise. Thus, it is desirable to point out major weaknesses in previous studies, as was done in Example 5.12.1.

Example 5.12.1

Despite the new information that O'Brien and Fassinger's (1993) work provided, their study had several limitations. For example, even though the researchers noted the importance of exploring the role of mothers in the career choices of young women, the model they tested did not address any maternal variables (e.g., employment status, educational status, gender role attitudes) previously identified as significant in the career development of women and adolescents. Second, the sample comprised seniors in an all-female private liberal arts school and, thus, was a select group. As O'Brien and Fassinger noted, their results might have limited generalizability to girls who have fewer educational and economic opportunities.[10]

---

[9] Wilson, Mason, & Ewing (1997, p. 317).
[10] Rainey & Borders (1997, pp. 160–161).

If a study is especially strong methodologically, you should consider mentioning it, especially when there are contradictory findings among the studies on your topic. Usually, you should give more weight to strong studies than to seriously flawed studies when reaching generalizations about the results of previous research.

➢ Guideline 5.13 Peripheral research may be cited in a thesis or dissertation when no literature with a direct bearing on the research topic can be located.

When Los Angeles first started implementing year-round school schedules, for example, there was no published research on the topic. There was research, however, on traditional school-year programs in which children attended school in shifts, on the effects of the length of the school year on achievement, and on the effectiveness of summer school programs. Students who were writing theses and dissertations on the Los Angeles program had to cite such peripheral literature in order to demonstrate their ability to conduct a search of the literature and write a comprehensive, well-organized review of literature. Remember that a thesis or dissertation is, in part, a test of a student's ability to locate, collect, and integrate references into a cohesive essay.

In a journal article, it would probably suffice to say that a systematic search of the literature revealed no studies on this topic.

➢ Guideline 5.14 Use direct quotations sparingly in literature reviews.

This guideline is suggested for three reasons. First, direct quotations often do not convey their full meaning when quoted out of context; quoting the context is usually less efficient than paraphrasing the main idea(s) of the author. Second, frequent quotations may disrupt the flow of the review because of the varying styles of the authors. Finally, quotations often bog the reader down in details that are not essential for the purpose of obtaining an overview of the literature. By paraphrasing, you can easily omit minor details.

Direct quotations are appropriate when the writer of the review (1) wants to illustrate either the original author's skill at writing or lack thereof or (2) believes that the wording of a statement will have an emotional impact on the reader that would be lost in paraphrase. These purposes seldom arise in presenting literature in an empirical research report.

➢ Guideline 5.15   Report sparingly on the details of the literature being cited.

Because the research being cited has usually been published, the reader can obtain copies to learn the details.

Typically, reviews of literature in theses and dissertations contain more details on cited research than reviews in journal articles. Even in theses and dissertations, however, the researcher should be selective in reporting details. For example, it may be appropriate to describe an especially important study in more detail than other, less important studies. Also, if your study builds directly on a previous study, it would be appropriate to discuss that study in detail so that your readers can see the connection between them.

➢ Guideline 5.16   Consider using literature to provide the historical context for the present study.

Following this guideline is especially desirable in theses and dissertations where students should demonstrate that they have a comprehensive knowledge of the literature on their topics. It is also appropriate in journal articles when researchers wish to (1) acknowledge the original proponents' theories and principles that underlie their current studies or (2) show that their research is a logical continuation of the historical chain of thought on a topic. Example 5.16.1 shows how the history of a topic might be briefly traced.

Example 5.16.1

As early as 1868, a German doctor, Von Dusch, noted that excessive work involvement and other behavioral characteristics seemed typical of people who develop CHD [coronary heart disease]. Similarly, Osler, in 1892, described the coronary-prone person as a "keen ambitious man, the indicator of whose engines are set at full speed ahead." Menninger and Menninger (1936) also emphasized the strong aggressive tendencies in CHD patients. In the 1940s and 1950s. . . .[11]

Concluding Comment

For many students, writing the introduction and review of literature is the most difficult part of writing an empirical research report. The guidelines in this chapter will help you avoid some major pitfalls; they do not, however, cover other important matters in effective writing such as providing clear transitions and writing with a sparse but clear style. The latter can be mastered only through guided learning under the tutelage of an experienced writer and through extensive reading of effective prose.

If you lack confidence in your ability to write introductions and literature reviews, follow these suggestions:

1. Write a topic outline as illustrated in Guideline 5.1, and take it with you when you consult with your instructor or committee. The outline will help them understand what you are trying to accomplish and make it easier for them to help you.

2. Read numerous reviews of literature, paying attention to how they are organized and how the authors make transitions from one topic to another.

3. After writing a first draft, have it reviewed by friends and colleagues— even if they are not experts on your topic. Ask them to point out elements that are not clear. Effective introductions are usually comprehensible to any intelligent lay person.

4. Be prepared to revise and rewrite. Because effective writing is achieved through this process, expect your instructor, committee, or journal editor to request revisions.

---

[11] Jamal & Baba (1991, pp. 1213–1214).

Exercise for Chapter 5

1. Examine the introductions to four journal articles on a topic of interest to you and answer the following questions.

   a. How many are organized according to Guideline 5.1?

   b. In how many does the author explicitly state why the research topic is significant? If any, copy one statement and bring it to class for discussion.

   c. In how many does the author use the first person? If any, copy an example and bring it to class for discussion.

   d. In how many is the literature review integrated with the introduction?

   e. In how many does the author express opinions on the quality of some of the research cited? If any, copy an example and bring it to class for discussion.

   f. In how many cases are direct quotations from the literature included?

   g. To what extent are details of previous research cited?

2. Examine the introductions and reviews of literature in four theses or dissertations. Answer questions *a* through *g* in question 1.

3. Write a topic outline for an introduction to a research project of interest to you. Have it reviewed by two friends or colleagues, and revise it in light of their comments. Bring the first and second drafts to class for discussion.

Chapter 6

Writing Definitions

Two types of definitions are usually found in empirical research reports. Conceptual definitions, which resemble dictionary definitions that refer to the general concepts, are often presented in the introduction. Operational definitions, which define traits in concrete, step-by-step physical terms, are usually presented in the section on methods.

In theses and dissertations, conceptual definitions are sometimes provided in a separate section of the introduction, with its own subheading. In journal articles, conceptual definitions are usually integrated into the introductory statement. Often, authors of journal articles assume that their readers are familiar with the general concepts and do not provide formal statements of conceptual definitions. In both types of reports, operational definitions should be provided in the section on research methods.

This chapter presents guidelines on what to define and how to write conceptual and operational definitions.

➤ Guideline 6.1   All variables in a research hypothesis, purpose, or question should be defined.

Example 6.1.1 is a hypothesis. "Newspaper reading habits" and "cultural literacy" need to be defined in the research report.

Example 6.1.1

There is a direct relationship between newspaper reading habits and cultural literacy.

➢ Guideline 6.2   A defining attribute of a population (also called a control variable) should be defined.

In Example 6.2.1, "adult education learners" is an attribute that should be defined.

Example 6.2.1
There is a direct relationship between newspaper reading habits and cultural literacy among adult education learners.

➢ Guideline 6.3   Theories and models on which the research is based should be defined.

The "deprivation model" mentioned in Example 6.3.1 should be defined. In a term project, thesis, or dissertation, a student may be expected to give a full, formal definition. In a journal article, a researcher may choose to provide an informal definition and refer the reader to a publication in which it is described in detail.

Example 6.3.1
In the introduction to a thesis, a student states:
The results will be discussed against the background of the deprivation model.

➢ Guideline 6.4   Conceptual definitions should be specific.

The definition of *therapists' self-disclosure* in Example 6.4.1 is not sufficiently specific. In the improved version, information is given on the elements that constitute self-disclosure. Note that it is perfectly acceptable to cite a definition previously offered by an expert (in this case, Mathews, 1989). In fact, this is often preferable to trying to devise a new way to define an established concept.

Example 6.4.1
Therapist self-disclosure involves the therapist disclosing personal information.

Improved Version of Example 6.4.1

Therapist self-disclosure is defined as the therapist revealing factual information about his or her life, revealing feelings he or she has experienced in his or her life, or revealing feelings he or she experiences regarding the client (Mathews, 1989).[1]

In Example 6.4.2, the author provides conceptual definitions in parentheses, which can be an effective technique for presenting brief conceptual definitions.

Example 6.4.2

To examine and compare men's and women's psychological separation from parents, I used Hoffman's (1984) model and the variables of functional independence (which focuses on one's ability to direct personal affairs without parental assistance), emotional independence (which taps one's reported freedom from excessive need for approval, closeness, and emotional support from parents), conflictual independence (which assesses one's reported freedom from guilt, anxiety, mistrust, and responsibility toward or resentment of one's parents), and attitudinal independence (which focuses on the maintenance of attitudes, values, and beliefs that differ from one's parents).[2]

➢ Guideline 6.5 Operational definitions should be provided. These are usually stated in the method section of a report or proposal.

An operational definition is one that is stated in terms of physical steps. After reading an operational definition, the reader should be able to see in his or her mind's eye the physical operations that were used to measure a variable, give treatments, define a population, or identify the relevant aspects of a model or theory.

In a study of the differences in female/male verbal behaviors, the authors of Example 6.5.1 provide operational definitions that refer to specific physical behaviors. Notice that they give examples, which help to operationalize the behaviors they are defining.

---

[1] Adapted from: Knox, Hess, Petersen, & Hill, (1997, p. 275).
[2] Lucas (1997, p. 124).

Example 6.5.1

Tag questions — a sentence with a declarative or imperative form with an interrogative dependent clause added on, for example, "It's a nice day, isn't it?"

Justifiers — evidence of reason given for a statement, for example, "I believe they should do it because it's a fair way to go."

Qualifiers — words that modify or soften the effect of what comes next, for example, "pretty good," "kind of fun," "almost correct."[3]

Example 6.5.2 is not operational because it does not describe the specific physical actions taken in the presence of the experimental subjects. This flaw has been corrected in the improved version.

Example 6.5.2

The stress-producing condition for the experimental group was a mild verbal threat given by the experimenter.

Improved Version of Example 6.5.2

In order to produce the stress-producing condition for the experimental group, a male experimenter dressed in a white doctor's jacket seated the subjects. He introduced himself as a medical doctor and stated that for the purposes of the experiment, "You will receive a mild electric shock while we measure your blood pressure."

➢ Guideline 6.6   For each conceptual definition, there should be a corresponding operational definition.

For each conceptual definition in the introduction, there should be an operational definition, usually in the method section. Example 6.6.1 illustrates this guideline.

Example 6.6.1

Conceptual definition in the introduction:

Ainsworth (1989)…and others (e.g., Sroufe & Waters, 1977) defined attachment as a meaningful and enduring emotional bond between two people. The secure attachment relationship was thought to provide the child with a sense of security, comfort, and predictability. Such a bond would be an important resource for children charting new developmental terrain.

---

[3] Turner, Dindia, & Pearson (1995, p. 90).

Corresponding operational definition in the method section:

ATTACHMENT TO PARENTS. The Parental Bonding Instrument (PBI; Parker, Tupling, & Brown, 1979) is a 50-item self-report questionnaire, with 25 items assessing relations with one's mother and the same 25 items assessing relations with one's father. The PBI yields a retrospective assessment of attachment bonds. Participants are instructed to recall their impressions of their parents, as formed during the first 16 years of their lives, and then to respond to items that reflect these impressions on a 4-point scale ranging from *very like my mother/father* (1) to *very unlike my mother/father* (4). Two dimensions of parent-child attachment are assessed by the PBI: care and protection.[4]

Notice that the authors of Example 6.6.1 have operationalized *attachment* by describing a published instrument used to measure the variable. This possibility is discussed under the next guideline.

➢ Guideline 6.7   If a published instrument was used, the variable measured by it may be operationally defined by citing the reference for the instrument.

A published instrument, such as an achievement test, almost always comes with specific, step-by-step directions for its use. By citing the test with a reference to the author and publisher, a researcher is providing an operational definition. Example 6.7.1 provides such a definition.

Example 6.7.1

Beginning mathematics skill was defined as the composite score on Form S of the Primary Level 2, multiple-choice/open-ended Mathematics Test of the Stanford Achievement Test Series, Ninth Edition (Harcourt Brace, 1997).

To further operationalize the definition in Example 6.7.1, the author could provide an overview of the physical properties of the test (e.g., content of the items, number of items, and time limits) and the statistical properties of the test, especially reliability and validity. This is a courtesy to the reader, who can also obtain this information by referring to a copy of the test and its manual.

---

[4] Rice, Cunningham, & Young (1997, p. 91).

➤ Guideline 6.8   If an unpublished instrument was used, the entire instrument should be reproduced in the report or a source for a copy of the instrument should be provided.

For specialized research purposes, researchers often have to construct their own instruments. If such an instrument is very short, a copy may be included as a figure in the research report. Longer instruments should be included in an appendix in a term project, thesis, or dissertation, but usually are not included in journal articles. Authors of journal articles should be prepared to supply copies of longer unpublished instruments to readers who request them. When it will not violate test security, providing sample items from the instrument in a research report is a good way to increase the operationalization of the variable measured with longer instruments.

➤ Guideline 6.9   Operational definitions should be sufficiently specific so that another researcher can replicate a study with confidence that he or she is examining the same variables under the same circumstances.

A replication is an attempt to reproduce the results of a previous study by using the same research methods. Replicability is the major criterion for judging the reliability of the results of empirical research. Inability to replicate results casts serious doubt on the validity of studies.

Even definitions that appear to be highly operational at first glance may be inadequate when one attempts to replicate a study. The definition in Example 6.9.1 illustrates this point. As one prepares to replicate a study involving this variable, questions about the physical process arise: How large were the letters? What type of screen was used? What type of film was used to produce the letters? and so on. Answers to these questions could easily affect individuals' ability to recognize letters of the alphabet.

Example 6.9.1

Visual acuity was defined as the ability to name the letters of the alphabet when flashed on a screen in a random order for a period of two seconds for each letter.

This guideline is often not followed to the letter. In practice, a writer must consider how operational a definition needs to be to permit a reasonably close replication. For making fine discriminations among very similar shapes, answers to the questions posed about Example 6.9.1 may be crucial to a successful replication.

➢ Guideline 6.10   Even a highly operational definition may not be a useful definition.

An operational definition that is too narrow or is too far afield from how others define a variable may be inadequate. Example 6.10.1 illustrates this point. It is fairly operational, but the definition of "self-concept" is much more narrow than that used by most psychologists and teachers.

Example 6.10.1

Self-concept was defined as the number of times each child smiled during the first 15 minutes of homeroom for five consecutive days. A smile was defined as a noticeable upward turn where the lips meet—based on agreement by three independent observers. Each observer was a graduate student in clinical psychology. Counts of smiles were made from videotapes, which permitted the observers to reexamine facial expressions that were questionable.

Concluding Comment

Writing satisfactory operational definitions is sometimes more difficult than it might appear at first. When writing them, assume that you are telling someone exactly how to conduct your study. Then have your definitions reviewed by colleagues and ask them if they could perform the same study in the same way without requesting additional information.

Exercise for Chapter 6

PART A: For each of the following definitions, describe what additional types of information, if any, are needed to make it fully operational.

1. Language skill was defined as scores on a scale from one to ten on essay tests that required students to write three essays in a 50-minute class period.

2. Depression was defined as the raw score on the Second Edition of the Beck Depression Inventory (Beck, 1996).

3. Computer phobia was defined as clear signs of anxiety when being seated in front of a computer.

4. Hispanic students were defined as those students whose surnames appeared on a master list of Hispanic/Latino/a surnames developed by the author in consultation with a linguist. This list may be obtained by writing to the author at P.O. Box xxx, Any City, State, Zip Code.

5. Potential high school dropouts were defined as those who have a poor attitude toward school.

PART B: For each of the following variables, write a highly operational definition. Because you may not have studied some of these variables, do not concern yourself with whether your definitions are highly useful (see Guideline 6.10).

6. Political involvement

7. Math anxiety

8. Welfare dependence

9. Ability to form friendships

10. Desire to achieve in school

PART C: Examine three research articles in journals and note how the variables are defined. Copy the definition you think is most operational and bring it to class for discussion.

PART D: Follow the directions for Part C, but examine three theses or dissertations.

PART E: Name a variable you might want to study. Write a conceptual definition and a highly operational definition of it. (For this activity, do not cite a published test or scale in order to define the variable you have selected.) Have the first draft of your definitions reviewed by colleagues and then revise them. Bring both drafts of the two definitions to class for discussion.

Notes:

Chapter 7

Writing Assumptions, Limitations, and Delimitations

An *assumption* is something that is taken to be true even though the direct evidence of its truth is either absent or very limited.

A *limitation* is a weakness or handicap that potentially limits the validity of the results. A *delimitation* is a boundary to which the study was deliberately confined. To understand the difference, consider a researcher who wants to study artistic creativity in general, but uses only a measure of creative drawing. This would be a limitation in the first sense because it is a weakness in the execution of the study. On the other hand, if the researcher only wants to study creative drawing and deliberately chooses a measure of this type of creativity, his or her findings would be delimited to this type of creativity, which is not a flaw in light of the researcher's purpose.

Authors of journal articles often integrate statements of assumptions, limitations, and delimitations in various sections of their articles, including the introduction, method section, and very frequently in the discussion section at the end of the report. These authors usually are very selective in deciding which ones to state, naming only those that are major. Students who are writing term projects, theses, and dissertations are often expected to discuss these issues in some detail in order to show that they understand these concepts. In theses and dissertations, the assumptions, limitations, and delimitations are often described in separate subsections of one of their chapters—often the first chapter.

➤ **Guideline 7.1   In the statement of an assumption, consider stating the reason(s) why it was necessary to make the assumption.**

In Example 7.1.1, this guideline has not been followed because while it states what was assumed, it does not state why the assumption was necessary. Because no measure of human behavior is perfectly valid, Example 7.1.1 adds little to the research report. In the first sentence of the improved version, the authors describe the circumstances that led to the use of a scale that may have limited validity.

Example 7.1.1

It was assumed that the cheerfulness scale was valid.

Improved Version of Example 7.1.1

Because we did not have the resources to make direct observations and ratings of cheerfulness over time in a variety of settings, we constructed a self-report measure of cheerfulness. It was necessary to assume that the participants were honest in reporting their typical levels of cheerfulness in their self-reports. To encourage honest responses, the cheerfulness scale was administered anonymously, and the participants were encouraged to be open and honest by the assistant who administered it.

➢ Guideline 7.2   If there is a reason for believing that an assumption is true, state the reason.

The last sentence in the Improved Version of Example 7.1.1 above suggests a basis for believing that the assumption is true. Likewise, the last sentence in Example 7.2.1 provides the basis for such a belief.

Example 7.2.1

Because the investigator could not be present in all the classrooms while the experimental method was being used, it was necessary to assume that the teachers consistently and conscientiously used the experimental method of instruction. This assumption seems tenable because the teachers were given intensive training in the method, as described in the method section of this report; and they reported enthusiasm for the method, as described in the results section.

➢ Guideline 7.3   If an assumption is highly questionable, consider casting it as a limitation.

Example 7.3.1 refers to a common flaw in research—a low response rate to a questionnaire. Unless a researcher has some empirical basis for believing that those who returned completed questionnaires are similar to those who did not, it would be better to describe this problem as a limitation, as is done in the improved version. Note that assumptions should not be used to "wish away" fundamental flaws.

Example 7.3.1

It is assumed that those graduate students who returned completed questionnaires by mail were similar on relevant variables to those who did not return them.

Improved Version of Example 7.3.1

There are some limitations to the findings of this study. The first deals with the problems associated with recruiting graduate students for participation in mail surveys. The choice of recruitment method used in this study resulted in the participation of 772 graduate students, but because the directors distributed the survey forms, the number of students who actually received the forms was unknown, and so the students' response rate of 35% was an approximation.[1]

➢ Guideline 7.4   Consider speculating on the possible effects of a limitation on the results of a study.

Example 7.4.1 illustrates this guideline; the authors speculate on the results that might have been obtained if the data had been collected anonymously.

Example 7.4.1

Given the nature of the interview, participants may have offered to discuss only what they considered socially acceptable chance events. Although the interviews were confidential, they were not anonymous. This limitation may account for the fact that only positive chance events were brought up by the participants.[2]

---

[1] Bernal, Sirolli, Weisser, Ruiz, Chamberlain, & Knight (1999, p. 54).
[2] Willams, Soeprapto, Like, Touradji, Hess, & Hill, (1998, p. 380).

➤ Guideline 7.5   Discuss limitations and delimitations separately.

Because they are separate issues, discuss the *limitations* (methodological weaknesses or flaws) in separate paragraphs or sections from *delimitations* (boundaries to which the study was deliberately limited). Example 7.5.1 points out a delimitation, while Example 7.5.2 describes some limitations of the same study.

Example 7.5.1

Background notes on a delimitation of a study:

For a study of the effects of a domestic violence treatment program, researchers *delimited* their study to participants who had been arrested for misdemeanor domestic violence offences. This was *not a limitation* (i.e., flaw) since the researchers were only interested in the effects of the treatment on participants who were mandated by the courts to attend the treatment program.

Example 7.5.2

Excerpt on the limitations of the study described in Example 7.5.1:

Other study limitations involve the sole reliance on police records [as an outcome measure]. Actual rates of recidivism are likely to be underreported in this study. We used police records of incident reports, arrests, and convictions for DV-related [domestic-violence related] offenses. However, a relatively small proportion of domestic violence incidents results in official charges.... We did not contact the victims to assess whether the batterers committed any [additional] violent offenses that were not reported to the police.... Without partner reports, we do not know how many men continued to be involved in relationships and thus even had an opportunity to reoffend over the two years post-arrest. Ideally, we would include partners' reports of batterers' violence as a measure of recidivism, in addition to using police records. Also, in this study, rates of threats and emotional abuse are unknown. It is possible....[3]

➤ Guideline 7.6   If a study is seriously flawed by important limitations, consider labeling it as a pilot study.

---

[3] Babcock & Steiner (1999, p. 53).

A pilot study is an exploratory study that is used to try out new instruments, see if subjects will be cooperative, check for preliminary support for a hypothesis, and so on. When this guideline is followed, it is usually done in the introduction as well as in the discussion at the end of the report.

Exercise for Chapter 7

1. Examine three theses or dissertations that contain explicit statements of assumptions. (Note that if there is a separate subsection containing assumptions, it will usually be listed in the Table of Contents.) How many assumptions were written in accordance with both Guidelines 7.1 and 7.2? If any, copy one and bring it to class for discussion. If none, copy an assumption and name the principle(s) that were not followed.

2. How many of the individual assumptions that you examined for question 1 involved generalizing from a sample to a population? How many involved the measuring tools or tests? How many involved the administration of experimental treatments? How many involved other issues? Name them.

3. Examine three theses or dissertations that contain explicit statements of limitations. In how many did the authors speculate on the possible effects of the limitations on the results of their studies? (Note: This type of speculation may appear in the final chapter.) If any, copy an example and bring it to class for discussion.

4. How many of the individual limitations that you examined for question 3 involved generalizing from a sample to a population? How many involved the measuring tools or tests? How many involved the administration of experimental treatments? How many involved some other issue?

5. Locate a statement of delimitations in a thesis or dissertation. Copy it and bring it to class for discussion.

6. Suppose you mailed a questionnaire to each member of a population but only 28% completed and returned it to you. Suppose you have no information on how the non-respondents differ from the respondents. Would you describe this circumstance as an assumption or as a limitation? Why?

7. Suppose you used a standardized test that had been validated for the type of population you were studying. Furthermore, suppose the test had high validity but, as with all tests, was somewhat less than perfectly valid. Would you describe this circumstance as an assumption or as a limitation? Why?

8. Suppose you administered both the experimental and control conditions to some experimental animals. You took extreme care to be sure that all animals were treated in the same way (e.g., diet, temperature, cage size, etc.) except for the administration of the treatments. Nevertheless, you realize that there is always the potential for human error no matter how careful a researcher tries to be. Would you state the fact that errors are always possible as an assumption, as a limitation, as a delimitation, or simply not refer to it in your research report? Why?

9. Consider a research project that you might plan to undertake. If you know of an assumption you would probably need to make, write a statement describing it.

10. Consider a research project you might plan to undertake. If you know of a limitation (i.e., methodological flaw) that you would probably have if you conducted the study, write a statement describing it. For the same study, describe a delimitation to which your study probably would be confined.

Chapter 8

Writing Method Sections

The section on methods contains a description of the physical steps taken to gather the data. Typically, it begins with a description of the individuals (such as schoolchildren) or objects (such as textbooks) you studied. Then the instrumentation (i.e., measuring tools) and any additional procedures, such as the administration of experimental treatments, should be described.

In reports on completed research, use the past tense to describe methods; in proposals, use the future tense.

➤ Guideline 8.1   Decide whether to use the term *subjects* or *participants* to refer to the individuals studied.

The traditional term for describing the individuals studied is *subjects*. Increasingly, researchers are using the term *participants* to refer to these individuals. The latter term conveys the idea that these individuals freely chose to take part in a research study.[1] We will consider these choices more fully under the next guideline.

➤ Guideline 8.2   Describe your informed consent procedures, if any, as well as steps taken to maintain confidentiality.

Institutions such as colleges and universities as well as funding sources such as government agencies often require researchers to obtain informed consent from the individuals who will be participating in

---

[1] Other terms that are sometimes used are *respondents* (e.g., to refer to those who respond to a mailed questionnaire) and *examinees* (e.g., to refer to those who are participating in test development research).

research studies. A consent form should be prepared that describes the purpose of the study, the possible benefits and harm that might result from participation, and identification of those who are conducting the research. Individuals are asked to sign the form acknowledging that they freely agree to participate and understand that they are free to withdraw from the study at any time without penalty.[2]

Example 8.2.1 illustrates how to briefly describe the use of informed consent in a research report. Note that the authors indicate that all those contacted signed the form. If the rate is less than 100%, this fact should also be mentioned.

Example 8.2.1

Registration [for participation in the study] was conditional on the person signing a consent form that indicated that he was over 18 years of age, knew he would be exposed to sexually explicit material, and knew, if he chose to be involved in the research study, that he could refuse to answer any question and could withdraw from the study at any time.... All participants signed the research form, and none refused any part of the questionnaire.[3]

Measures taken to protect the rights of participants to confidentiality are described in Example 8.2.2. Also notice that permission from the parents of minors was obtained.

Example 8.2.2

Initially, each [school] district assisted in the construction of the parent permission form and accompanying letter to convey the importance of the study and the district's support.... A standard set of administration and collection procedures was given to all test administrators. These procedures prevented administrators from approaching students during the administration and from determining student identification from the collection sequence. Confidentiality measures also included preventing teachers and other nonresearch personnel from identifying students by name or number, and hand carrying sensitive data from the school to the data-collection location.[4]

When individuals freely consent to participate in a study, it seems logical to call them *participants*. Of course, informed consent is not always obtained. For example, if you were conducting an observational study of the behavior of adolescents in a large shopping mall, you might

---

[2] Obtain precise guidelines for preparing an informed consent form from your institution or funding agency.
[3] Ross & Rosser (1996, p. 17).
[4] Jenkins (1996, p. 300).

find that you don't need consent to observe these public behaviors (although it would still be highly desirable to maintain confidentiality in your data handling procedures). In such a study, the term *subjects* seems more appropriate because the individuals are not knowingly participating and, of course, have not consented to participate.

➤ Guideline 8.3   The participants should be described in enough detail for the reader to visualize them.

Example 8.3.1 helps readers visualize the participants' ethnicity, age, place of residence (i.e., urban residents), and income. Note that the symbol *n* stands for *number of cases*.

Example 8.3.1

The sample of 1,203 pregnant women was drawn from two public prenatal clinics in Texas and Maryland. The ethnic composition was African American ($n = 414$, 34.4%), Hispanic, primarily Mexican American ($n = 412$, 34.2%), and White ($n = 377$, 31.3%). Most women were between the ages of 20 and 29 years; 30% were teenagers. All were urban residents, and most (94%) had incomes below the poverty level as defined using each state's criteria for Women, Infants, and Children (WIC) eligibility.[5]

Because the number of characteristics of participants that might be used to describe them is almost limitless, researchers must be highly selective in deciding on which ones to report. As a general rule, describe those that are most relevant to the issues being studied. For example, in a study on physician's attitudes toward assisted suicide, "religious background" would be a relevant demographic variable. For a study on algebra achievement, it would not be relevant.

Tables such as the one in Example 8.3.2 make it easy for readers to scan the information on the participants. Note the use of the term *demographic characteristics* in the title of the table. These are background characteristics that help readers visualize the participants.

---

[5] McFarlane, Parker, & Soeken (1996, p. 38).

Example 8.3.2

Table 8.3.2 *Demographic characteristics of the participants*

Characteristic	Number	Percent
Gender		
Girl	81	72
Boy	31	28
Current grade level		
Third	16	14
Fourth	37	33
Fifth	55	49
Sixth	4	4
Family status		
Living with both parents	72	64
Living with one parent	35	31
Living with neither parent	5	4

➢ Guideline 8.4   When a sample is very small, consider providing a description of individual participants.

After summarizing in general terms the ages and psychiatric histories of ten participants in their study, the authors of Example 8.4.1 presented a table providing information on each individual. A portion of the table is shown in Example 8.4.1.

Example 8.4.1

Client	Age	Sex	Psychiatric Diagnosis
1	25	M	Conduct disorder
			Attention deficit disorder
			Learning disability
2	19	M	Dysthymic disorder
			Major depression
3	22	F	Learning disability
4	30	F	Major depression
Etc.			

➢ Guideline 8.5   A population should be named, and if only a sample was studied, the method of sampling should be described.

Example 8.5.1 illustrates this guideline.

Example 8.5.1

From the population of all seniors enrolled in high schools in the Los Angeles Unified School District, 250 were selected at random.

When a researcher fails to name a population, it is usually safe to assume that he or she used a sample of convenience. Example 8.5.2 illustrates this common problem.

Example 8.5.2

Undergraduate students ($N = 195$; $n = 92$ women; $n = 103$ men) from the University of Texas at Austin volunteered for the study if they met the requirement of having a same-gender sibling in the age range of 13–17 and agreed that their parents and younger sibling could be contacted.[6]

When the method of sampling is clearly deficient, such as the one in Example 8.5.2, it is a good idea for the author to acknowledge this fact with a phrase such as "Because a sample of convenience was used, generalizations to populations should be made with extreme caution," or "The use of volunteers greatly restricts the generalizability of the results." Inclusion of statements such as these is especially important in student projects, theses, and dissertations. In their absence, instructors may not know whether students are aware of this important limitation.[7]

➢ Guideline 8.6   If there was attrition, state the number who dropped out, the reasons for attrition, if known, and information on the dropouts, if available.

Example 8.6.1 illustrates this guideline.

---

[6] D'Amico & Fromme (1997, p. 428).

[7] While statements regarding generalizing from a sample are often made in the Method section, many researchers make them in the Discussion section at the end of the research report.

Example 8.6.1

Two boys (ages 10 and 11) and three girls (all age 10) dropped out of the study because their families had moved out of the school district. All five were Latino/a and spoke English as a second language. Their percentile ranks on the *Metropolitan Reading Test* (English Version) ranged from 30 to 45, which is similar to the percentile ranks of the participants who did not drop out.

➢ Guideline 8.7   Unpublished instruments should be described in detail.

Instruments are measuring tools (such as achievement tests, attitude scales, questionnaires, and interview schedules). The instrument used to measure a construct defines it. For example, if a researcher is studying attitudes toward capitalism, the items on her attitude scale constitute her definition of this type of attitude. If another researcher uses a different set of items to measure attitudes toward capitalism, he will have a different definition of this construct than the first researcher. Obviously, it is important to provide readers with detailed information on the instruments, including the items when possible.

Frequently researchers have to build their own instruments because none are available for their particular research purposes. When this is done, the section on methods should provide a detailed description of the instrument. Consider Example 8.7.1, which has insufficient detail, and its improved version. Notice that the researcher has included the questionnaire in an appendix, which is desirable when space permits.

Example 8.7.1

Attitude toward school was measured with a nine-item questionnaire developed for use in this study.

Improved Version of Example 8.7.1

Attitude toward school was measured with a questionnaire developed for use in this study. It contains nine statements. The first three measure attitudes toward academic subjects; the next three measure attitudes toward teachers, counselors, and administrators; the last three measure attitudes toward the social environment in the school. Participants were asked to rate each statement on a five-point scale from 1 (strongly disagree) to 5 (strongly agree). The questionnaire is shown in Appendix A.

➤ Guideline 8.8   If a published instrument was used, briefly describe the traits that it was designed to measure, its format, and the possible range of score values.

There is less obligation for a researcher to describe in detail a published instrument than an unpublished instrument because published instruments are usually available for inspection by other researchers. Nevertheless, as a courtesy to their readers, researchers should provide some general information about published instruments, such as those elements suggested in this guideline.

➤ Guideline 8.9   For both unpublished and published instruments, information on reliability and validity, when available, should be reported.

The two most important characteristics of an instrument are its reliability (consistency of results) and validity (whether the instrument measures what it is designed to measure). For published instruments that are well-known and in widespread use, it is sometimes sufficient to refer only briefly to the availability of reliability and validity information in other published sources such as journal articles and test manuals. This was done in the last sentence of Example 8.9.1.

Example 8.9.1

Self-reported communication behavior was assessed with the Communication Patterns Questionnaire (CPQ; Christensen & Shenk, 1991), a 23-item inventory in which each partner rates the extent to which they use each of a number of common patterns of couple communication in managing conflict, such as demand-withdraw and mutual avoidance (Christensen & Shenk, 1991). The scale has been used extensively in recent couples research and has established reliability and validity (Christensen, 1988; Christensen & Heavey, 1990).[8]

---

[8] Sanders, Halford, & Behrens (1999, p. 65).

For less well-known published as well as unpublished instruments, more detail on these issues is desirable, which is illustrated in Example 8.9.2.

Example 8.9.2

Overall psychological distress as well as three subdimensions of psychological distress were measured by a 30-item version of the Hopkins Symptom Checklist (HSCL; Derogatis, Lipman, Rickels, Uhlenhuth, & Covi, 1974). . . . Derogatis et al. reported internal consistency reliability coefficients ranging from .84 to .87 for each of the three subscales, and test-retest reliability estimates ranging from .75 to .82 over a 1-week interval. . . . Evidence supporting the construct validity of the HSCL has been reported by Rickels, Lipman, Garcia, & Fisher (1972) in a study comparing parents' distress levels on the symptom dimensions with ratings by clinical practitioners.[9]

Students who are writing theses and dissertations may be expected to describe the reliability and validity of the instruments they use in considerable detail. They may be expected, for example, to summarize how the reliability and validity studies were conducted and to interpret the results of these studies in light of any methodological flaws they may have had.

➢ Guideline 8.10   Experimental procedures, equipment, and other mechanical matters should be described in sufficient detail so that the study can be replicated.

Some subjectivity enters into the decision as to how much detail to provide; in most cases, authors of journal articles do not provide every detail. Instead, they try to provide enough information to permit a reasonably close replication. Example 8.10.1 shows a description that might permit a rough replication.

Example 8.10.1

The massage therapy group received a massage 2 days a week for 5 weeks, for a total of 10 massages. The massages were administered by massage therapists. The massage therapy covered several parts of the body (which was fully clothed) and included 15 minutes in a supine position and 15 minutes in a prone position.

---

[9] Ingram, Corning, & Schmidt (1996, p. 221).

It consisted of exerting traction upon the neck with the patient in a supine position, followed by smooth strokes across the forehead, jaw, and face, and depressing the shoulders. The therapist then exerted traction on each arm followed by....[10]

Generally, more detail on experimental procedures, equipment, and other mechanical matters are expected in term projects, theses, and dissertations than in journal articles because students are expected to show that they can write precise, detailed descriptions.

Exercise for Chapter 8

1. Locate a description of participants or subjects that is highly detailed (i.e., contains sufficient demographic information so that you can visualize the participants or subjects). Bring it to class for discussion.

2. Locate a description of participants or subjects that lacks sufficient detail. Copy it and briefly describe other types of information that might have been included to give a better picture of the subjects.

3. Examine the descriptions of participants or subjects in three research reports. In how many did the authors explicitly name a population and a specific method of sampling? If any, select the one you think is best and bring it to class for discussion.

4. Locate a description of the instrumentation that describes its reliability and validity. Bring it to class for discussion.

5. Locate a description of instrumentation that lacks sufficient information. Copy it and briefly describe other types of information that might have been included to provide a more complete description.

6. Examine the description of procedures in the three sources that you used for question 3. Copy the one that is most detailed. Briefly describe whether you think it is sufficiently detailed and why.

---

[10] Field, Schanberg, Kuhn, Field, Fierro, Henteleff, Mueller, Yando, Shaw, & Berman (1998, p. 557).

Notes:

Chapter 9

Writing Analysis and Results Sections

The analysis and results section usually follows the section on methods. In a proposal, the proposed method of analysis should be described; the anticipated results may also be discussed.

> **Guideline 9.1   Organize the analysis and results section around the research hypotheses, purposes, or questions stated in the introduction.**

Example 9.1.1 shows the three research questions posed in the introduction to a research report on economically disadvantaged preschoolers. It also shows a portion of the results. Notice how the results are organized around the three research questions.

Example 9.1.1

Research questions posed in the introduction:

The research was guided by three questions: (a) Is frequency of television viewing associated with the school readiness of preschoolers from economically disadvantaged homes? (b) Is frequency of television viewing related to quality of home environment such as maternal instruction, books in the home, and mother-child reading? (c) Is parental employment related either to television viewing time or to the educational quality in the home?

Portions of the results section, which illustrate the organization around research questions:

Our first research question concerned the relationship between viewing time and school readiness. Correlational analysis with age and IQ covaried revealed that television viewing time was negatively related to school readiness. . . .

To address the second research question, we calculated Pearson product-moment correlations between television viewing time and home environment variables. These analyses indicated that children's television viewing time was significantly negatively related to parental instruction $r(28) = -.351$ and. . . .

The third research question concerned parental employment. Consistent with prior research, our correlational analyses indicated that. . . .[1]

➢ Guideline 9.2 Standard statistical procedures need only be named; you do not need to show formulas or calculations.

Likewise, it is usually unnecessary to name the particular computer program used to perform the analysis.

➢ Guideline 9.3 The scores of individual participants usually are not shown; instead, statistics based on them should be reported.

Suppose you had tested a random sample of 50 students in an elementary school with a standardized achievement test battery. Normally, you would *not* list the scores of individual children. Instead, you would provide summary statistics such as the mean and standard deviation. Note, however, that some instructors may require students who are writing term projects, theses, and dissertations to include participants' scores in an appendix so that the instructor can check the analysis.

➢ Guideline 9.4 Present descriptive statistics first.

For each set of continuous scores, provide information on central tendency and variability (usually means and standard deviations) before presenting correlation coefficients, if any, and the results of inferential statistical tests. For example, correlation coefficients may provide direct information on a research hypothesis; even if this is the case, report measures of central tendency and variability first. These measures will

---

[1] Clarke & Kurtz-Costes (1997, pp. 281–282).

show your reader what the average participant was like and how variable the group was.

For categorical (nominal) data, present frequencies and percentages before presenting the results of inferential statistical tests.

➢ Guideline 9.5 Organize large numbers of statistics in tables and give each table a number and descriptive title (i.e., caption).

Tables are especially effective for helping readers compare groups. The table in Example 9.5.1 makes it easy to compare the ages of women and men.

Example 9.5.1

Table 9.5.1 *Percentages of women and men in various age groups*

Age	Women ($n = 830$)	Men ($n = 723$)
18 years and under	4.8% ($n = 40$)	8.7% ($n = 63$)
19–24 years	9.9% ($n = 82$)	13.3% ($n = 96$)
25–34 years	18.2% ($n = 151$)	25.4% ($n = 184$)
35–44 years	22.8% ($n = 189$)	19.4% ($n = 140$)
45–54 years	20.0% ($n = 166$)	15.4% ($n = 111$)
55–64 years	13.7% ($n = 114$)	13.8% ($n = 100$)
65–74 years	5.3% ($n = 44$)	2.6% ($n = 19$)
75 years and over	5.3% ($n = 44$)	1.4% ($n = 10$)
Total	100.0%	100.0%

The titles of tables (also known as *captions*) should name the statistics presented in the table and refer to the variables that were measured. Example 9.5.2 shows four titles that do this.

Example 9.5.2

Table 1 *Number of Participants by Gender and Grade Level*

Table 2 *Means and Standard Deviations on Reading and Mathematics*

Table 3 *Analysis of Variance for Reading Scores*

Table 4 *Analysis of Variance for Mathematics Scores*

When separate tables are presented for two or more groups, the title of each table should also name the group. Example 9.5.3 shows the titles of tables for two different groups.

Example 9.5.3

Table 1 *Intercorrelation Matrix of Middle-Level Managers' Personality Scores*

Table 2 *Intercorrelation Matrix of Chief Executive Officers' Personality Scores*

➢ Guideline 9.6   When describing the statistics presented in a table, point out highlights for the reader.

Briefly describe the important points in each table you present. Because the values of the statistics are presented in a table, it is not necessary to repeat each value in your discussion of the results. This is illustrated in Example 9.6.1, which shows a statistical table, and Example 9.6.2, which shows the discussion of it.

Example 9.6.1

Table 9.6.1 *Percentage of Inhalant Use of Local Sample Compared with National Sample*

Grade	Lifetime		Past Year		Past Month	
	Local	National	Local	National	Local	National
8	21.7	17.4	13.1	9.5	7.6	4.7
10	17.9	16.6	13.1	7.5	6.0	2.7

Note. National sample data from Johnston, O'Malley, & Bachman, 1993.

Example 9.6.2

Table 9.6.1 shows a comparison of the local school population and the national sample. Reports of past month's use by 8th-grade and 10th-grade students in the local sample were much higher than those reported by 8th-grade and 10th-grade students in the national sample (Johnston et al., 1993). The percentage of local students who reported past month and past year use of inhalants was about double that of the national statistics, for 10th-graders particularly.[2]

---

[2] McGarvey, Canterbury, Cohn, & Clavet (1996, pp.183–184).

> ## Guideline 9.7   Statistical figures (i.e., drawings such as histograms) should be professionally drawn; they should be used sparingly in journal articles.

Figures may be used to organize and describe data; they usually take up more space, however, than would a corresponding statistical table. Because space in journals is at a premium, figures should be used sparingly. In term projects, theses, and journals, where space is not limited, they may be used more frequently.

Because figures attract the eye better than tables, their best use is to present important data—especially striking data that might otherwise be overlooked in a table of statistical values. Example 9.7.1 shows such a figure, which illustrates these striking differences: White models are exposed more frequently in White magazines while Black models are exposed more frequently in Black magazines.

Example 9.7.1

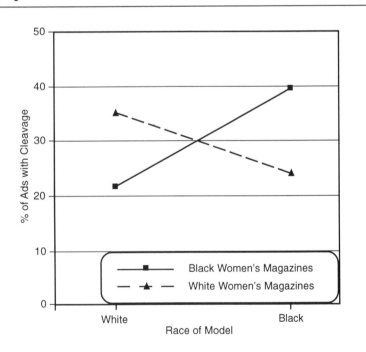

Figure 4

The percentage of advertisements with breast or cleavage exposure, broken down by the race of female models and the race of magazine readership.[3]

---

[3] Plous & Neptune (1997, p. 641).

➢ Guideline 9.8   Statistical symbols should be underlined or italicized.

In Example 9.8.1, the statistical symbols (i.e., *t*, *df*, and *p*) are italicized. If you do not have the ability to italicize, underline the symbols; typesetters recognize underlining as a direction to italicize.

Example 9.8.1

The mean of the experimental group was significantly higher than the mean of the control group ($t = 2.310$, $df = 10$, $p < .05$, two tailed).

➢ Guideline 9.9   Use the proper case for each statistical symbol.

As statistical symbols, upper- and lower-case letters often have different meanings. For example, a lower-case *f* stands for "frequency," while an upper-case *F* is an inferential statistic used in significance testing.

➢ Guideline 9.10   Spell out numbers that are less than ten. Spell out numbers that start sentences.

The main exceptions to this guideline are when referring to elements in a numbered list such as "Chapter 1" and "Chapter 2" and when presenting precise numerical results (e.g., "The median equals 1.").

➢ Guideline 9.11   Qualitative results should be organized and the organization made clear to the reader.

In qualitative studies, statistics are usually not reported. Instead, researchers report on major trends and themes that emerged from subjective analyses of data such as transcribed interviews. The presentation of such results should be organized; consider using subheadings to guide the reader through the results. This is illustrated in Example 9.11.1, which is the first paragraph in the results section of a report on a qualitative study. Each of the five italicized terms was used as a subheading in the results section.

Example 9.11.1

The present study resulted in an emergent theoretical model for understanding the career development of high-achieving African American–Black and White women.... The emergent model postulates a *core story*, consisting of participants' career behaviors, attitudes toward work, and relationships in both professional and personal life, that is enacted within *sociocultural*, *personal background*, and *current contextual conditions*; in addition, *actions and consequences* result and, in turn, cycle back to exert influence on the contextual conditions, thus creating a dynamic, constantly evolving person-environment interaction.[4]

See Chapter 12 for additional guidelines on reporting the results of qualitative research.

Exercise for Chapter 9

1. Examine the results sections of two published articles. Determine whether the authors followed Guideline 9.4. Be prepared to discuss your findings in class.

2. Locate a statistical table in a published article that you think has a good title (i.e., caption). Copy it and bring it to class for discussion.

3. Locate a statistical figure in a published article and discuss whether presentation in the form of a table of statistical values would have been as effective as the figure.

---

[4] Richie, Fassinger, Linn, Johnson, Prosser, & Robinson (1997, p. 137).

Notes:

Chapter 10

Writing Discussion Sections

This chapter presents guidelines for writing the last section of a journal article or the last chapter of a thesis or dissertation. This section or chapter typically begins with one of various headings such as *Summary and Discussion*, *Discussion and Conclusions*, or simply *Discussion*.

➢ Guideline 10.1 Consider starting the discussion with a summary.

Authors of long research reports, theses, and dissertations often begin their discussion section with a summary of the highlights of the material that preceded it. For short reports, a summary is usually not necessary.

➢ Guideline 10.2 In the discussion, refer to the research hypotheses, purposes, or questions stated in the introduction.

Indicate whether the data support the hypotheses, whether the purposes were achieved, or what answers were obtained for the research questions. Of course, you did this in the results section — probably in some detail with a number of statistics. In the discussion, do not repeat all the details—just reiterate the highlights, as was done in Example 10.2.1, which is the beginning of a discussion section in a research report.

Example 10.2.1

The first purpose of this study was to assess faculty-student interactions and students' perceptions for sex differences. In our sample of 24 college classrooms,

81

no main or interaction effects for student sex on the faculty-student behaviors were observed, suggesting that men and women participated at similar rates in their classrooms.[1]

➤ Guideline 10.3   Point out the extent to which results of the current study are consistent with the results in the literature reviewed in the introduction.

Since the review of the literature near the beginning of a research report helps set the stage for the current study, it is important to discuss at the end how the current findings relate to those reported earlier in the literature. This is illustrated in Example 10.3.1 in which the researchers note consistency with other research as well as with theory. In Example 10.3.2, the researcher notes that the results are inconsistent with suggestions found in the literature.

Example 10.3.1

One gender difference that did emerge, as we predicted, was that wives in aggressive marriages tend to perceive their husband's aggression as motivated by a wish to control them, whereas this was reported significantly less often by husbands. This finding is consistent with other research in which men describe their own marital aggression as instrumentally motivated (Hamberger, 1993). The finding is also consistent with social control theory, which posits that aggression is used as a means of redressing perceived deviations for expectations. For instance, Gondolf (1985) observed that aggressive husbands often become aggressive in response to a perception that their wives failed to fulfill a role obligation.[2]

Example 10.3.2

Theorists who suggest that the existence and meaning of gender differences in aggression may vary across cultures (Burbank, 1994; Fry & Gabriel, 1994...) will not find evidence to support this belief in the present study. Instead, these findings are consistent with those suggesting that greater aggressiveness by males is found in a variety of cultures and subcultures (Bjorkqvist, 1994; Burbank, 1992, Daly and Wilson, 1988...).[3]

---

[1] Brady & Eisler (1999, p. 138).
[2] Ehrensaft, Langhinrichsen-Rohling, Heyman, O'Leary, & Lawrence (1999, p. 30).
[3] Harris (1996, p. 861).

➢ Guideline 10.4   Consider interpreting the results and offering explanations for them in the discussion section.

Following this guideline helps readers understand the results and put them in context. Since interpretations and explanations go beyond the data actually collected, researchers should be careful not to imply that they are data-based explanations; rather, they are possible explanations that are consistent with the data. The authors of Example 10.4.1 offer two explanations for one of their findings.

Example 10.4.1

Women with substance abuse problems were less likely to have social support from family members, particularly their parents. There are two possible explanations for this finding. First, women with a history of substance abuse may have alienated family members because of their drug-related behaviors. Second, these women may have fewer family resources to draw on because of the substance abuse of family members.[4]

It is especially helpful to offer explanations for unexpected findings. In Example 10.4.2, the researchers were surprised to find that residential instability did not predict behavior problems in a sample of children age six and older.

Example 10.4.2

To our surprise, residential instability did not predict behavior problems and, in fact, children who had moved more often in the past year were less likely to have either internalizing or externalizing behavior problems.... Although not a definitive finding, a possible explanation is that some children may habituate to residential instability and be less affected by moving to a shelter than children who have experienced greater housing stability prior to becoming homeless.[5]

➢ Guideline 10.5   Consider mentioning important strengths and limitations in the discussion.

Strengths and limitations of the research methodology are sometimes first mentioned in the introduction or section on methods. Because

---

[4] Marcenko & Spence (1995, p. 108).
[5] Buckner, Bassuk, Weinreb, & Brooks (1999, p. 253).

strengths and limitations can affect the interpretations of data described in the discussion section, it is often appropriate to mention them again. The authors of Example 10.5.1 suggest that their findings be interpreted with caution because of two limitations. Notice that the authors speculate on the possible effects of the limitations on the validity of the results.

Example 10.5.1

In interpreting the present results, readers should consider several limitations to this study. First, only fifth-grade students from one elementary school participated. It may be difficult to generalize these results to other age groups. For example, younger students might have had more difficulty interacting and staying on task in cooperative group activities. In addition, mathematics was used as the content area for this study. These results might not necessarily transfer to other subject areas such as language arts, science, or social studies. Writing activities, for example, generally take longer to complete than do math problems. Students might have more difficulty completing this type of activity in cooperative groups because of the personal nature of many writing activities.[6]

By pointing out that a study is especially strong methodologically, researchers encourage their readers to give more credence to their study. Example 10.5.2 shows a statement regarding the strengths of a study.

Example 10.5.2

Overall, the study has several strengths. First, data were obtained from mothers, fathers, and the children, so that each of their perspectives could be examined separately. Second, we tested predicted associations with some positive, as well as the more commonly studied negative, aspects of marital conflict. Studies of the role of constructive marital conflict in facilitating positive child functioning, not just the absence of behavior problems or distress, have been neglected.[7]

➢ Guideline 10.6   It is usually inappropriate to introduce new data or new references in the discussion section.

The final section of a research report should be used to summarize and interpret what was presented earlier. The introduction of new data or references distracts from this purpose.

---

[6] Brush (1997, p. 62).
[7] Goodman, Barfoot, Frye, & Belli (1999, p. 44).

➢ Guideline 10.7   When possible, explicitly state the implications of the results in the discussion section.

The implications of a study are usually cast in the form of actions that individuals or organizations should take based on the results of the study. The last sentence in Example 10.7.1 describes a specific implication.

Example 10.7.1

The present intervention has financial implications for communities as well. It has been estimated that women make approximately 1.5 million medical visits per year to treat injuries sustained by male partners and ex-partners (Straus, 1986). When one calculates the cost involved in this, added to the criminal justice system costs, employment-related costs, child protective services costs, and social service delivery costs, it becomes clear that intimate male violence against women is a tremendous financial burden to communities. It is notable, then, that women [in this study] who received advocacy services were more than twice as likely to remain completely free from intimate violence across a 2-year time period. Given the low expense involved in training and supervising paraprofessionals [used in this study], this type of intervention is extremely cost-effective.[8]

In Example 10.7.2, the authors also state an implication.

Example 10.7.2

This analysis has shown that when maltreatment becomes more serious, the child is at a statistically significant risk of a wide variety of school performance declines. Investigating the magnitude of this risk shows that the increase is moderate in size. These findings imply that effective intervention may shield children from this moderately increased risk, an implication open to empirical investigation. . . .[9]

If you have conducted a pilot study, you probably should hedge a bit in your statement of implications by beginning the statement with a caution such as the one shown in Example 10.7.3.

Example 10.7.3

If the results obtained in this pilot study are confirmed in more definitive studies, the following implications should be considered by. . . .

---

[8] Sullivan & Bybee (1999, p. 50).
[9] Leiter & Johnsen (1997, p. 586).

In a proposal, you should discuss the possible implications of the study. Sometimes this is done in the introduction, and sometimes it is done in a separate section at the end of the proposal. Example 10.7.4 shows how this might begin.

Example 10.7.4

If the research hypothesis is supported by the data collected in the proposed study, the implications will be. . . .

➤ Guideline 10.8   Be specific when making recommendations for future research.

It is uninformative to end a research report with a vague statement such as "Further research is needed." Instead, researchers should point out what specific directions this research might take in order to advance knowledge of a topic. Example 10.8.1 illustrates the degree of specificity often found in journal articles.

Example 10.8.1

Future research is needed to determine the extent to which these results generalize to couples who are separated or divorced, refuse to participate in a study on marriage, have never been married, or have been married for much longer periods of time, or where the aggression is so severe as to motivate the wife to seek protection at a battered women's shelter. Also, given the small sample size, particularly of the DNA (distressed nonaggressive) group, replication of the study would be important.[10]

Exercise for Chapter 10

1. Read three research articles published in journals, and examine the discussion sections of them carefully.

   a. In how many do the authors discuss the consistency of their results with previously published results?

---

[10] Ehrensaft, Langhinrichsen-Rohling, Heyman, O'Leary, & Lawrence (1999, p. 31).

b. In how many do the authors mention important strengths and weaknesses of their studies?

c. In how many do the authors introduce new data or new references?

d. In how many do the authors explicitly state the implications of the results?

2. Compare the three discussion sections you examined for question 1, and select the one you think is the best. Copy it and bring it to class for discussion.

3. Read a research report published in a journal, but do not read the discussion section. Write a discussion section for it, and then compare yours with the one written by the author(s) of the article.

Notes:

Chapter 11

Writing Abstracts

An abstract is a summary of the report that is placed below the title in a journal article. In a thesis or dissertation, it is usually placed on a separate page following the title page.

➤ Guideline 11.1   In the abstract, refer to the research hypotheses, purposes, or questions.

Researchers often begin their abstracts with very brief statements of their research hypotheses, purposes, or questions. This was done in Example 11.1.1, which shows the beginning of an abstract.

Example 11.1.1
The purpose of the present research was to design an innovative instructional method for teaching mathematics in heterogeneous classrooms (with no tracking) and to investigate its effects on students' mathematics achievement. The method is based on....[1]

➤ Guideline 11.2   Highlights of the methodology should be summarized.

Information on methodology (such as whether a survey was conducted with a national sample or only a local sample) helps potential readers determine whether the report will be of interest to them. Example 11.2.1 shows a complete abstract. Notice that the second through fifth sentences describe research methodology.

---

[1] Mevarech & Kramarski (1997, p. 365).

Example 11.2.1

The primary focus of this study was to determine the effectiveness of a classwide peer tutoring program for three learner types: low achievers, with and without disabilities, and average achievers. Twelve schools, stratified on student achievement and family income, were assigned randomly to experimental and control groups. Twenty teachers implemented the peer tutoring program for 15 weeks; 20 did not implement it. In each of the 40 classrooms, data were collected systematically on three students representing the three learner types. Pre- and post-treatment reading achievement data were collected on three measures of the Comprehensive Reading Assessment Battery. Findings indicated that, irrespective of type of measure and type of learner, students in peer tutoring classrooms demonstrated greater reading progress. Implications for policymaking are discussed.[2]

➢ Guideline 11.3   Highlights of the results should be included in the abstract.

In Example 11.2.1 above, the results are mentioned in the next to the last sentence. In Example 11.3.1, the abstract provides a more detailed description of the results. Notice that the authors of both examples begin with reference to their purpose, followed by information on their research methods, and end with information on their results. This arrangement is recommended.

Example 11.3.1

This study is an attempt to determine the literature preferences of fourth grade boys and girls. The purpose of the study is to assist teachers in promoting reading by selecting literature that these children prefer to read. A fictitious-annotated-titles survey was used to determine reading preferences in ten fiction and eleven nonfiction categories, and to determine the effect of gender of main characters on reading preference. A sample stratified by type of school district was randomly selected from the elementary schools in Ohio. The final sample included 211 girls and 194 boys. Both boys and girls were found to prefer fiction more strongly than nonfiction. The girls preferred fiction more strongly than the boys, and the boys preferred nonfiction more strongly than the girls. The boys preferred male main characters more strongly than the girls. The girls preferred female main characters more strongly than the boys.[3]

---

[2] Fuchs, Fuchs, Mathes, & Simmons (1997, p. 174).
[3] Harkrader & Moore (1997, p. 325).

➢ Guideline 11.4   An abstract should usually be short; however, there are exceptions.

Many journals limit the number of words that may be included in abstracts—some as short as 100. Example 11.4.1 shows the suggested organization for a short abstract. Other journals encourage long abstracts. Students who are writing theses and dissertations should determine their institution's requirements regarding length and number of words. When long abstracts are permitted (or required), consider also incorporating information on the importance of the problem and the implications of the results in addition to the other elements mentioned in the earlier guidelines in this chapter. In a long abstract, you may want to use subheadings such as those shown in Example 11.4.2.

Example 11.4.1

Suggested elements to cover in a short abstract (no subheadings):

1. Research hypotheses, purposes, or questions. These may need to be abbreviated or summarized if they are extensive.
2. Highlights of the research methods.
3. Highlights of the results.

Example 11.4.2

Suggested elements to cover in a long abstract (subheadings shown in italics):

1. *Background*
   Describe the problem area and its importance.
2. *Research Hypotheses*
   (or *Research Purposes* or *Research Questions*)
3. *Method*
4. *Results*
5. *Implications*

The amount of emphasis to put on each element in an abstract is a subjective matter. When writing it, keep in mind that your goal is to provide enough information for potential readers to make informed decisions on whether to read your research report. Elements that make your research unique generally deserve more emphasis than other elements. For example, if you are the first to conduct a true experiment on a problem, emphasize that point and include some information on how you conducted your experiment.

Exercise for Chapter 11

1. Locate an abstract for a journal article that you believe illustrates the four guidelines in this chapter. Bring a copy to class for discussion.

2. Locate a research report published in a journal, and read the article without reading the abstract. Write your own abstract for the article and compare it with the abstract prepared by the author of the article.

Chapter 12

A Closer Look at Writing Reports of Qualitative Research

With certain obvious exceptions such as some of the guidelines on reporting statistical results, the guidelines in the previous chapters should be considered when writing reports of qualitative research. This chapter presents guidelines that are specific to reporting qualitative research.

➤ Guideline 12.1   Consider using the term "qualitative" in the title or abstract of the report.

Because the vast majority of research in the social and behavioral sciences continues to be *quantitative*, using the term *qualitative* in a title or abstract helps interested readers locate qualitative research. Examples 12.1.1 and 12.1.2 show how some researchers have used the term in titles.

Example 12.1.1

Turning Points in the Lives of Young Inner-City Men Forgoing Destructive Criminal Behaviors: A Qualitative Study[1]

Example 12.1.2

Sexual Attraction Toward Clients, Use of Supervision, and Prior Training: A Qualitative Study of Predoctoral Psychology Interns[2]

Notice that in both of the above titles, the term *qualitative* was used near the end of the titles, which seems appropriate since most readers searching for research reports are probably more interested in the variables studied (e.g., "Sexual Attraction Toward Clients") than in the methodological approach employed by researchers.

---

[1] Hughes (1998, p. 143).
[2] Ladany, O'Brien, Hill, Melincoff, Knox, & Petersen (1997, p. 413).

Note that this guideline is more important when the qualitative research has been conducted on a topic that has traditionally been approached quantitatively since the use of qualitative methodology on such a topic is a distinguishing characteristic of the research.

Also note that using terms traditionally associated with qualitative research such as "in-depth interviews," "focus groups," and "participant observation" in an abstract will help readers identify the research as qualitative.

➢ Guideline 12.2 In the introduction, consider discussing the choice of qualitative over quantitative methodology.

This guideline is especially recommended if you will be presenting your research to an audience that is quantitatively oriented such as readers of a journal that usually publishes quantitative research. Example 12.2.1 illustrates this guideline. In it, the researchers point out that little is known about their topic, making it inappropriate to attempt to impose the high level of structure (such as specific hypotheses and structured questionnaires) that would be required if the topic were investigated quantitatively.[3]

Example 12.2.1

Because we know so little about the role of chance events in women's career development, it seemed appropriate to use a qualitative approach to explore the topic. Qualitative research methods have recently gained greater attention for their contributions to the existing and mostly quantitative psychological literature…. Qualitative research is useful for examining an issue or experience from the framework of the participants, without making judgments in advance as to what results one may find.[4]

Example 12.2.2 also illustrates Guideline 12.2.

---

[3] Note that while qualitative methods are often more appropriate than quantitative methods for investigating new problem areas, this discussion is not meant to imply that qualitative methods should be employed only for new topics.
[4] Williams, Soeprapto, Like, Touradji, Hess, & Hill (1998, p. 380).

Example 12.2.2

Because the purpose of the current study is to explore mothers' perceptions of the impact of homelessness and shelter life on their relationships with their children, the qualitative research paradigm was selected as most appropriate. Qualitative methodology is particularly useful in studying families because of the emphasis on meanings, interpretations, interactions, and subjective experiences of family members (Daly, 1992; Gilgun, 1992). The theoretical underpinnings of the qualitative research paradigm in family research are phenomenology and symbolic interactionism. Phenomenology attempts to "understand the meaning of events and interactions...and the subjective aspects of people's behavior" (Bogdan & Bicklen, 1992, p. 34). Symbolic interactionism asserts that "human experience is mediated by interpretation.... Objects, people, situations, and events do not possess their own meaning, rather meaning is conferred on them" (Bogdan & Bicklen, 1992, p. 36). Thus, to understand how homelessness and shelter life might impact family relations, it is important to explore the subjective experience of families within the context of homelessness and how mothers interpret and make meaning of that experience.[5]

➢ Guideline 12.3   Consider describing the qualitative method or approach used in the research.

Having stated that the research is qualitative and the reasons for selecting a qualitative approach, it is desirable to describe the particular approach that was used. This is especially important when addressing a quantitatively oriented audience or when using a relatively new qualitative approach. Example 12.3.1 shows the beginning of such a description. Note that material of this type may be included in the introduction or in the methods section of a report.

Example 12.3.1

We used the consensual qualitative approach (CQR) methodology developed by Hill, Thompson, and Williams (in press).... According to Hill et al. (in press) the key features of this approach are the following: (a) The method relies on words to describe phenomena rather than using numbers; (b) a small number of cases is studied intensively; (c) the context of the whole case is used to understand the parts of the experience; (d) the process is inductive, with theory being built from observations of data rather than....[6]

---

[5] Lindsey (1998, p. 245).
[6] Knox, Hess, Petersen, & Hill (1997, p. 277).

➢ Guideline 12.4   Consider "revealing yourself" to your reader.

While quantitative researchers are taught to be "objective" and distance themselves from their research to avoid influencing the outcome, qualitative researchers recognize the inherently subjective nature of research. In addition, most qualitative researchers use methods that involve personal interactions such as in-depth interviews, participant observation, and focus groups. Because of the personal nature of qualitative research, it is often appropriate for researchers to describe themselves to their readers. Example 12.4.1 shows an example provided by researchers in the report on a study of single (not married) women. When such descriptions are provided, they are usually included in the introduction or methods section of a report.

Example 12.4.1

The first author has a master's in social work and an Ed.D. in counseling psychology. She is a clinical member of AAMFT and an approved supervisor. She has over 28 years experience as both a family and a group therapist. She became interested in the subject of single women from two perspectives. As a clinician, she had noted dramatic changes in the ways her single heterosexual women clients spoke about men over the past two decades. Her single female clients, from a wide range of ages, ethnic backgrounds, and economic situations, were raising similar questions and concerns about their inability to establish gratifying romantic relationships. In addition, as a woman who has always been single herself (now 51 years old), she was struck by the parallels between what she was hearing from clients and what seemed like a sequence of issues she had tackled and/or continues to tackle in her own life. She felt that the time was ripe to conduct a study exploring the women's perspectives on their singleness.

The second author has a Ph.D. in educational psychology and is a clinical member of AAMFT. She has 6 years of experience as a family therapist and 10 years of experience as a single again woman and single parent. She was interested in working on the project because....[7]

➢ Guideline 12.5   Avoid calling a sample "purposive" if it is really a sample of convenience.

---

[7] Lewis & Moon (1997, p. 121).

A *purposive* sample is one that is believed to be especially well suited for obtaining meaningful data on a particular research problem. In other words, it is a group of participants that a researcher selects because they have characteristics that make them especially worthy of attention.

When researchers use participants who are selected simply because they are convenient (such as students who happen to be enrolled in a professor's psychology course), the sample should be identified as one of convenience—not purposive—by using a phrase such as "a sample of convenience" or "accidental sample."

➤ Guideline 12.6   If a purposive sample was used, state the basis for selection of participants.

In Example 12.6.1, the researchers describe a sample that was purposively selected to be diverse, yet include only schools and programs in which children with disabilities were included in regular school activities.

Example 12.6.1

We used a purposive sampling procedure to maximize variation among the programs (Lincoln & Guba, 1985), selecting community-based, public school, and Head Start Programs from rural, suburban, and urban settings across the nation. The programs varied considerably in their approach to including young children with disabilities; however, teachers and administrators identified their program as inclusive. One constant across all programs was that children with and without disabilities participated in joint activities.[8]

➤ Guideline 12.7   Consider describing how participants were recruited.

Whether a sample of convenience or a purposive sample was used, readers are likely to be interested in how the participants were recruited.[9]

---

[8] Lieber, Capell, Sandall, Wolfberg, Horm, & Beckman (1998, pp. 89, 91).

[9] Of course, this also applies to quantitative research except in the case where researchers use the textbook model for participant selection: Define a population, identify those who belong to it, and select participants at random.

This is especially true when studying potentially sensitive issues because poor recruitment procedures may lead to highly atypical samples. Example 12.7.1 shows portions of a longer, detailed description of the recruitment of mothers who were HIV-positive.

Example 12.7.1

Every effort was made to recruit women into the study who were not receiving services from agencies, as well as those who were known to the services system.... The recruitment procedure varied by site and was determined in large part by staff suggestions and mutual concerns about client confidentiality. At four of the sites, agency staff recruited women to participate.... At one health program, the social worker asked HIV-positive mothers who were patients of the program for permission to be contacted by the researcher.... The women who attended the group at the needle-exchange program learned of the focus groups through one of several mechanisms: Flyers describing the focus group were distributed....[10]

➢ Guideline 12.8   Consider providing details on how the data were collected.

In an interview study, it is usually insufficient to state merely that "in-depth, semistructured interviews were conducted." Readers will want to know where and how the interviews were conducted as well as some general directions the initial questions took. Example 12.8.1 illustrates this. Note that it is not necessary to state the actual questions used (especially since the questions may vary somewhat from participant to participant and may be changed over the course of a qualitative study in light of the data collected from earlier participants).

Example 12.8.1

Interviews took place in offices or the participants' homes with no other people present. The interviews began by my verifying that each participant met the criteria. Then I collected demographic data (age, ethnicity, marital and parental status, education level attained, employment status, and place of residence). The remainder of the first interviews focused on open-ended, topical questions concerning experiences with family, school, law enforcement and criminal justice, significant people, intervention programs, community, street group affiliation (if applicable), and significant life events. I chose these topics to ensure that the participants covered significant life stages and agents contributing

---

[10] Marcenko & Samost (1999, pp. 37–38).

to their socialization. I asked the participants to detail those periods and events related to their decisions to make positive changes in their life course.[11]

Providing details on data collection is also desirable when reporting on observational studies. Consider answering questions such as these when writing the description: Was the observer a participant or nonparticipant? When were the observations made? How often were they made? How were the data recorded? For what types of behaviors did the researcher initially look?

➢ Guideline 12.9   In the results section, report quantitative results on quantitative matters.

Doing qualitative research does not preclude the use of statistics when they are appropriate. Some matters naturally lend themselves to quantification. Note that the term "many" in Example 12.9.1 is a vague quantitative term. The improved version is more specific.

Example 12.9.1

Many of the students were observed to have their heads down on their desks during the mathematics lesson.

Improved Version of Example 12.9.1

About 25% of the students were observed to have their heads down on their desks during the mathematics lesson.

➢ Guideline 12.10   If quotations are reported, consider stating the basis for their selection.

In qualitative research, large amounts of narrative material (the raw data) are often collected. Readers will be interested in learning the basis for your selection of the limited number of quotations you present in your results section. Note that there may be different reasons for the selection of the various quotations. Some might be selected because they are the

---

[11] Hughes (1998, p. 146).

most articulate expressions of a recurring theme. Others might be selected because they are the most emotional. Still others might be presented to illustrate a typical response to some topic.

Arguably, the most common basis for selecting quotations is because they are somehow "typical" or "representative." When making this claim about quotations, consider indicating *how* typical they are by indicating the number and percentage of participants who expressed similar sentiments. Example 12.10.1 illustrates this. In the example, the researcher states the category of the finding, followed by the number of transcripts and percentage in which it was found, followed by quotations from participants illustrating the categories.

Example 12.10.1

CLIENT TRUSTS THERAPIST (11 transcripts, 100% of transcripts)

"The fact that I've been able to trust her...."

"I totally, totally trust her...."

CLIENT FEELS LISTENED TO (6 transcripts, 55% of transcripts)

"I think in general it was just so helpful to have her there to listen. Somebody who listens...."

"I feel so heard when she says back to me what I'm saying to her. I love that...."[12]

Note that Example 12.10.1 is taken out of context from a report in which the meanings of the categories and quotations are discussed. The results section of a qualitative report should *not* consist merely of a listing of categories and the associated percentages. Instead, they should be interpreted and discussed in terms of the points they illustrate.

➤ Guideline 12.11   If two or more researchers participated in analyzing the data, discuss how they arrived at a consensus.

Questions that might be addressed in light of this guideline are: Did the researchers analyze the data independently and then confer, or did they analyze it together from the beginning? If there were disagreements on

---

[12] Phelps, Friedlander, & Enns (1997, p. 328).

some aspects of the interpretation, how were they resolved? How confident does each researcher feel in the final interpretations presented in the report?

➤ Guideline 12.12   Consider discussing alternative interpretations of the data and why they were rejected.

If there are obvious alternative interpretations that are likely to come to readers' minds, the reasons for rejecting them should be explicitly discussed. For example, a researcher might use quotations or talk about trends in the data that run counter to the alternatives, which would help explain why one interpretation was selected over another.

Concluding Comment

Writing effective reports of both qualitative and quantitative research is an art that can be mastered only with practice and careful modeling of the writing of skilled professionals. To move beyond this book and become a true master of empirical research writing, the most important thing you can do is *read, read, read* the research written by others—with attention to detail, style, and mechanics. Skimming articles or, worse yet, reading only the abstracts is not sufficient. Instead, you should read research reports in their entirety while evaluating them by asking questions such as: What makes a report effective or ineffective? At what points did you get lost while reading a report? What else could the researcher have done to assist you in following his or her line of reasoning? In short, by becoming a critical consumer of research written by others, you will become a skilled writer of empirical research.

Exercise for Chapter 12

Locate two or more reports of qualitative research. Determine the extent to which each one illustrates the application of the guidelines in this chapter. Bring them to class for discussion.

References

Babcock, J. C. & Steiner, R. (1999). The relationship between treatment, incarceration, and recidivism of battering: A program evaluation of Seattle's coordinated community response to domestic violence. *Journal of Family Psychology*, *13*, 46–59.

Bernal, M. E., Sirolli, A. A., Weisser, S. K., Ruiz, J. A., Chamberlain, V. J., & Knight, G. P. (1999). Relevance of multicultural training to students' applications to clinical psychology programs. *Cultural Diversity and Ethnic Minority Psychology*, *5*, 43–55.

Brady, K. L. & Eisler, R. M. (1999). Sex and gender in the college classroom: A quantitative analysis of faculty-student interactions and perceptions. *Journal of Educational Psychology*, *91*, 127–145.

Browne, B. A. (1997). Gender and beliefs about workforce discrimination in the United States and Australia. *The Journal of Social Psychology*, *137*, 107–116.

Buckner, J. C., Bassuk, E. L., Weinreb, L. F., & Brooks, M. G. (1999). Homelessness and its relation to the mental health and behavior of low-income school-age children. *Developmental Psychology*, *35*, 246–257.

Brush, T. A. (1997). The effects on student achievement and attitudes when using integrated learning systems with cooperative pairs. *Educational Technology Research and Development*, *45*, 51–64.

Burnette, D. (1999). Custodial grandparents in Latino families: Patterns of service use and predictors of unmet needs. *Social Work*, *44*, 22–34.

Clarke, A. T. & Kurtz-Costes, B. (1997). Television viewing, educational quality of the home environment, and school readiness. *The Journal of Educational Research*, *90*, 279–285.

Cook, C. A. L., Selig, K. L., Wedge, B. J., & Gohn-Baube, E. A. (1999). Access barriers and the use of prenatal care by low-income, inner-city women. *Social Work*, *44*, 129–139.

D'Amico, E. J. & Fromme, K. (1997). Health risk behaviors of adolescent and young adult siblings. *Health Psychology*, *16*, 426–432.

De Gaston, J. F., Weed, S. & Jensen, L. (1996). Understanding gender differences in adolescent sexuality. *Adolescence*, *31*, 217–231.

Ehrensaft, M. K., Langhinrichsen-Rohling, J., Heyman, R. E., O'Leary, K. D., & Lawrence, E. (1999). Feeling controlled in marriage: A phenomenon specific to physically aggressive couples? *Journal of Family Psychology*, *13*, 20–32.

Field, T., Schanberg, S., Kuhn, C., Field, T., Fierro, .K., Henteleff, T., Mueller, C., Yando, R., Shaw, S., & Burman, I. (1998). Bulimic adolescents benefit from massage therapy, *Adolescence*, *33*, 555–563.

Fuchs, D., Fuchs, L. S., Mathes, P. G., & Simmons, D. C. (1997). Peer-assisted learning strategies: Making classrooms more responsive to diversity. *American Educational Research Journal*, *34*, 174–206.

Goodman, S. H., Barfoot, B., Frye, A. A., & Belli, A. M. (1999). Dimensions of marital conflict and children's social problem-solving skills. *Journal of Family Psychology*, *13*, 33–45.

Grunberg, L., Moore, S., Anderson-Connolly, R., & Greenberg, E. (1999). Work stress and self-reported alcohol use: The moderating role of escapist reasons for drinking. *Journal of Occupational Health Psychology*, *4*, 29–36.

Harkrader, M. A. & Moore, R. (1997). Literature preferences of fourth-graders. *Reading Research and Instruction*, *36*, 325–339.

Harris, M. B. (1996). Aggressive experiences and aggressiveness: Relationship to ethnicity, gender, and age. *Journal of Applied Social Psychology*, *26*, 843–870.

Hill, C. E., Diemer, A., & Heaton, K. J. (1997). Dream interpretation sessions: Who volunteers, who benefits, and what volunteer clients view as most and least helpful. *Journal of Counseling Psychology*, *44*, 53-62.

Hughes, M. (1998). Turning points in the lives of young inner-city men forgoing destructive criminal behaviors: A qualitative study. *Social Work Research*, *22*, 143–151.

Ickovics, J. R., Druley, J. A., Morrill, A. C., Grigorenko, E., & Rodin, J. (1998). "A grief observed": The experience of HIV-related illness and death among women in a clinic-based sample in New Haven, Connecticut. *Journal of Consulting and Clinical Psychology*, *66*, 958–966.

Ingram, K. M., Corning, A. F., & Schmidt, L. D. (1996). The relationship of victimization experiences to psychological well-being among homeless women and low-income housed women. *Journal of Counseling Psychology, 43,* 218–227.

Jamal, M., & Baba, V. V. (1991). Type A behavior, its prevalence and consequences among women nurses: An empirical examination. *Human Relations, 44,* 1213–1228.

Jenkins, J. E. (1996). The influence of peer affiliation and student activities on adolescent drug involvement. *Adolescence, 31,* 297–306.

Knox, S., Hess, S. A., Petersen, D. A., & Hill, C. E. (1997). A qualitative analysis of client perceptions of the effects of helpful therapist self-disclosure in long-term therapy. *Journal of Counseling Psychology, 44,* 274–283.

Knudson-Martin, C. & Mahoney, A. R. (1998). Language and processes in the construction of equality in new marriages. *Family Relations, 47,* 81–91.

Koff, E. & Bauman, C. L. (1997). Effects of Wellness, Fitness, and Sport-Skills Programs on Body Image and Lifestyle Behaviors. *Perceptual and Motor Skills, 84,* 555–562.

Ladany, N., O'Brien, K. M., Hill, C. E., Melincoff, D. S., Knox, S., & Petersen, D. A. (1997). Sexual attraction toward clients, use of supervision, and prior training: A qualitative study of predoctoral psychology interns. *Journal of Counseling Psychology, 44,* 413–424.

Landrine, H., Klonoff, E. A., & Alcaraz, R. (1997). Racial discrimination in minors' access to tobacco. *Journal of Black Psychology, 23,* 135–147.

Leiter, J., & Johnsen, M. C. (1997). Child maltreatment and school performance declines: An event-history analysis. *American Educational Research Journal, 34,* 563–589.

Lewis, K. G. & Moon, S. (1997). Always single and single again women: A qualitative study. *Journal of Marital and Family Therapy, 23,* 115–134.

Lieber, J., Capell, K., Sandall, S. R., Wolfberg, P., Horm, E., & Beckman, P. (1998). Inclusive preschool programs: Teachers' beliefs and practices. *Early Childhood Research Quarterly, 13,* 87–105.

Lindsey, E. W. (1998). The impact of homelessness and shelter life on family relationships. *Family Relations, 47,* 243–252.

Lucas, M. (1997). Identity development, career development, and psychological separation from parents: Similarities and differences between men and women. *Journal of Counseling Psychology, 44,* 123–132.

Marcenko, M. O. & Samost, L. (1999). Living with HIV/AIDS: The voices of HIV-positive mothers. *Social Work, 44,* 36–45.

Marcenko, M. O. & Spence, M. (1995). Social and psychological correlates of substance abuse among pregnant women. *Social Work Research, 45,* 37–42.

McFarlane, J., Parker, B., & Soeken, K. (1996). Abuse during pregnancy: Associations with maternal health and infant birth weight. *Nursing Research, 45,* 37–42.

McGarvey, E. L., Canterbury, R. J., Cohn, W. F., & Clavet, G. J. (1996). Adolescent inhalant use and school problems. *The School Counselor, 43,* 181–186.

Mevarech, Z. R., & Kramarski, B. (1997). IMPROVE: A multidimensional method for teaching mathematics in heterogeneous classrooms. *American Educational Research Journal, 34,* 365–394.

Phelps, A., Friedlander, M. L., & Enns, C. Z. (1997). Psychotherapy process variables associated with the retrieval of memories of childhood sexual abuse: A qualitative study. *Journal of Counseling Psychology, 44,* 321–332.

Plous, S. & Neptune, D. (1997). Racial and gender biases in magazine advertising: A content-analytic study. *Psychology of Women Quarterly, 21,* 627–644.

Purdie, N., & Hattie, J. (1996). Cultural differences in the use of strategies for self-regulated learning. *American Educational Research Journal, 33,* 845–871.

Rainey, L. M., & Borders, D. (1997). Influential factors in career orientation and career aspiration of early adolescent girls. *Journal of Counseling Psychology, 44,* 160–172.

Rice, K. G., Cunningham, T. J., & Young, M. B. (1997). Attachment to parents, social competence, and emotional well-being: A comparison of Black and White late adolescents. *Journal of Counseling Psychology, 44,* 89–101.

References

Richie, B. S., Fassinger, R. E., Linn, S. G., Johnson, J., Prosser, J., & Robinson, S. (1997). Persistence, connection, and passion: A qualitative study of the career development of highly achieving African American–Black and White women. *Journal of Counseling Psychology, 44*, 133–148.

Ross, M. W. & Rosser, B. R. S. (1996). Measurement and correlates of internalized homophobia: A factor analytic study. *Journal of Clinical Psychology, 52*, 15–21.

Sanders, M. R., Halford, W. K., & Behrens, B. C. (1999). Parental divorce and premarital couple communication. *Journal of Family Psychology, 13*, 60–74.

Slonim-Nevo, V. Auslander, W. F., Ozawa, M. N., & Jung, K. G. (1996). The long-term impact of AIDS-preventive interventions for delinquent and abused adolescents. *Adolescence, 31*, 409–421.

Sparapani, E. F., Abel, F. J., Easton, S. E., Edwards, P., & Herbster, D. L. (1997). Cooperative learning: An investigation of the knowledge and classroom practice of middle-grades teachers. *Education, 118*, 251–258.

Stafford, L. & Kline, S. L. (1996). Married women's name choices and sense of self. *Communication Reports, 9*, 85–92.

Stasz, C. & Brewer, D. J. (1998). Work-based learning: Student perspectives on quality and links to school. *Educational Evaluation and Policy Analysis, 20*, 31–46.

Strage, A. & Brandt, T. S. (1999). Authoritative parenting and college students' academic adjustment and success. *Journal of Educational Psychology, 91*, 146–156.

Sullivan, C. M. & Bybee, D. I. (1999). Reducing violence using community-based advocacy for women with abusive partners. *Journal of Consulting and Clinical Psychology, 67*, 43–53.

Sweet, A. P., Guthrie, J. T., & Ng, M. M. (1998). Teacher perceptions and student reading motivation. *Journal of Educational Psychology, 90*, 210-223.

Turner, L. H., Dindia, K., & Pearson, J. C. (1995). An investigation of female/male verbal behaviors in same-sex and mixed-sex conversations. *Communication Reports, 8*, 86–96.

Williams, E. N., Soeprapto, E., Like, K., Touradji, P., Hess, S., & Hill, C. E. (1998). Perceptions of serendipity: Career paths of prominent academic women in counseling psychology. *Journal of Counseling Psychology, 45*, 379–389.

Wilson, S. B., Mason, T. W., & Ewing, M. J. M. (1997). Evaluating the impact of receiving university-based counseling services on student retention. *Journal of Counseling Psychology, 44*, 316–320.

Notes:

Appendix A

Checklist of Guidelines

Instructors may wish to refer to the following checklist numbers when commenting on students' papers (e.g., "See Principle 5.2"). Students can use this checklist to review important points as they prepare their research reports and proposals.

Chapter 1 Writing Simple Research Hypotheses

____ 1.1 A simple research hypothesis should name two variables and indicate the type of relationship expected between them.

____ 1.2 When a relationship is expected only in a particular population, reference to the population should be made in the hypothesis.

____ 1.3 A simple hypothesis should be as specific as possible, yet expressed in a single sentence.

____ 1.4 If a comparison is to be made, the elements to be compared should be stated.

____ 1.5 Because most hypotheses deal with the behavior of groups, plural forms should usually be used.

____ 1.6 A hypothesis should be free of terms and phrases that do not add to its meaning.

____ 1.7 A hypothesis should indicate what will actually be studied—not the possible implications of a study or value judgments of the author.

____ 1.8 A hypothesis usually should name variables in the order in which they occur or will be measured.

____ 1.9 Avoid using the words "significant" or "significance" in a hypothesis.

____ 1.10 Avoid using the word "prove" in a hypothesis.

____ 1.11 Avoid using two different terms to refer to the same variable in a hypothesis.

____ 1.12 Avoid making precise statistical predictions in a hypothesis.

Chapter 2 A Closer Look at Hypotheses

____ 2.1 A "statement of the hypothesis" may contain more than one hypothesis. It is permissible to include them in a single sentence as long as the sentence is reasonably concise and its meaning is clear.

____ 2.2 When a number of related hypotheses are to be stated, consider presenting them in a numbered or lettered list.

____ 2.3 The hypothesis or hypotheses should be placed before the section on methods.

____ 2.4 It is permissible to use terms other than the term "hypothesis" to refer to a hypothesis.

____ 2.5 In a research report, a hypothesis should flow from the narrative that immediately precedes it.

____ 2.6 A hypothesis may be stated without indicating the type of relationship expected between variables. To qualify as a hypothesis, however, it must specify that some unknown type of relationship is expected.

____ 2.7 When a researcher has a research hypothesis, it should be stated in the research report; the null hypothesis need not always be stated.

Chapter 3 Writing Research Purposes, Objectives, and Questions

____ 3.1 When the goal of research is to describe group(s) without describing relationships among variables, write a research purpose or question instead of a hypothesis.

____ 3.2 When there is insufficient evidence to permit formulation of a hypothesis regarding a relationship between variables, write a research purpose or question.

____ 3.3 The research purpose or question should be as specific as possible, yet stated concisely.

____ 3.4 When a number of related purposes or questions are to be stated, consider presenting them in a numbered or lettered list.

____ 3.5 In a research report, a research purpose or question should flow from the narrative that immediately precedes it.

Chapter 4 Writing Titles

____ 4.1 If only a small number of variables are studied, the title should name the variables.

____ 4.2 If many variables are studied, only the *types* of variables should be named.

____ 4.3 The title of a journal article should be concise; the title of a thesis or dissertation may be longer.

____ 4.4 A title should indicate what was studied—not the results or conclusions of the study.

____ 4.5 Mention the population(s) in a title when the type(s) of populations are important.

____ 4.6 Consider the use of subtitles to amplify the purposes or methods of study.

____ 4.7 A title may be in the form of a question; this form should be used sparingly and with caution.

____ 4.8 In titles, use the words "effect" and "influence" with caution.

____ 4.9 A title should be consistent with the research hypothesis, purpose, or question.

____ 4.10 Consider mentioning unique features of a study in its title.

____ 4.11 Avoid clever titles, especially if they fail to communicate important information about the report.

Chapter 5 Writing Introductions and Literature Reviews

____ 5.1 Start the introduction by describing the problem area; gradually shift its focus to specific research hypotheses, purposes, or questions.

____ 5.2 Start long introductions and literature reviews with a paragraph that describes their organization, and use subheadings to guide readers.

____ 5.3 The importance of a topic should be explicitly stated in the introduction to a term paper, thesis, or dissertation.

____ 5.4 A statement on the importance of a topic should be specific to the topic investigated.

____ 5.5 Use of the first person is acceptable; it should be used when it facilitates the smooth flow of the introduction.

____ 5.6 The literature review should be presented in the form of an essay—not in the form of an annotated list.

____ 5.7 The literature review should emphasize the findings of previous research—not just the research methodologies and names of variables studied.

____ 5.8 Point out trends and themes in the literature.

____ 5.9 Point out gaps in the literature.

____ 5.10 Consider pointing out the number or percentage of people who are affected by the problem you are studying.

____ 5.11 Point out how your study differs from previous studies.

____ 5.12 Feel free to express opinions about the quality and importance of the research being cited.

____ 5.13 Peripheral research may be cited in a thesis or dissertation when no literature with a direct bearing on the research topic can be located.

____ 5.14 Use direct quotations sparingly in literature reviews.

____ 5.15 Report sparingly on the details of the literature being cited.

____ 5.16 Consider using literature to provide the historical context for the present study.

Chapter 6 Writing Definitions

____ 6.1 All variables in a research hypothesis, purpose, or question should be defined.

____ 6.2 A defining attribute of a population (also called a control variable) should be defined.

____ 6.3 Theories and models on which the research is based should be defined.

____ 6.4 Conceptual definitions should be specific.

____ 6.5 Operational definitions should be provided. These are usually stated in the method section of a report or proposal.

____ 6.6 For each conceptual definition, there should be a corresponding operational definition.

___ 6.7 If a published instrument was used, the variable measured by it may be operationally defined by citing the reference for the instrument.

___ 6.8 If an unpublished instrument was used, the entire instrument should be reproduced in the report or a source for a copy of the instrument should be provided.

___ 6.9 Operational definitions should be sufficiently specific so that another researcher can replicate a study with confidence that he or she is examining the same variables under the same circumstances.

___ 6.10 Even a highly operational definition may not be a useful definition.

Chapter 7 Writing Assumptions, Limitations, and Delimitations

___ 7.1 In the statement of an assumption, consider stating the reason(s) why it was necessary to make the assumption.

___ 7.2 If there is a reason for believing that an assumption is true, state the reason.

___ 7.3 If an assumption is highly questionable, consider casting it as a limitation.

___ 7.4 Consider speculating on the possible effects of a limitation on the results of a study.

___ 7.5 Discuss limitations and delimitations separately.

___ 7.6 If a study is seriously flawed by important limitations, consider labeling it as a pilot study.

Chapter 8 Writing Method Sections

___ 8.1 Decide whether to use the term *subjects* or *participants* to refer to the individuals studied.

___ 8.2 Describe your informed consent procedures, if any, as well as steps taken to maintain confidentiality.

___ 8.3 The participants should be described in enough detail for the reader to visualize them.

___ 8.4 When a sample is very small, consider providing a description of individual participants.

___ 8.5 A population should be named, and if only a sample was studied, the method of sampling should be described.

___ 8.6 If there was attrition, state the number who dropped out, the reasons for attrition, if known, and information on the dropouts, if available.

___ 8.7 Unpublished instruments should be described in detail.

___ 8.8 If a published instrument was used, briefly describe the traits that it was designed to measure, its format, and the possible range of score values.

___ 8.9 For both unpublished and published instruments, information on reliability and validity, when available, should be reported.

___ 8.10 Experimental procedures, equipment, and other mechanical matters should be described in sufficient detail so that the study can be replicated.

Chapter 9 Writing Analysis and Results Sections

____ 9.1 Organize the analysis and results section around the research hypotheses, purposes, or questions stated in the introduction.

____ 9.2 Standard statistical procedures need only be named; you do not need to show formulas or calculations.

____ 9.3 The scores of individual participants usually are not shown; instead, statistics based on them should be reported.

____ 9.4 Present descriptive statistics first.

____ 9.5 Organize large numbers of statistics in tables and give each table a number and descriptive title (i.e., caption).

____ 9.6 When describing the statistics presented in a table, point out highlights for the reader.

____ 9.7 Statistical figures (i.e., drawings such as histograms) should be professionally drawn; they should be used sparingly in journal articles.

____ 9.8 Statistical symbols should be underlined or italicized.

____ 9.9 Use the proper case for each statistical symbol.

____ 9.10 Spell out numbers that are less than ten. Spell out numbers that start sentences.

____ 9.11 Qualitative results should be organized and the organization made clear to the reader.

Chapter 10 Writing Discussion Sections

____ 10.1 Consider starting the discussion with a summary.

____ 10.2 In the discussion, refer to the research hypotheses, purposes, or questions stated in the introduction.

____ 10.3 Point out the extent to which results of the current study are consistent with the results in the literature reviewed in the introduction.

____ 10.4 Consider interpreting the results and offering explanations for them in the discussion section.

____ 10.5 Consider mentioning important strengths and limitations in the discussion.

____ 10.6 It is usually inappropriate to introduce new data or new references in the discussion section.

____ 10.7 When possible, explicitly state the implications of the results in the discussion section.

____ 10.8 Be specific when making recommendations for future research.

Chapter 11 Writing Abstracts

____ 11.1 In the abstract, refer to the research hypotheses, purposes, or questions.

____ 11.2 Highlights of the methodology should be summarized.

____ 11.3 Highlights of the results should be included in the abstract.

___ 11.4 An abstract should usually be short; however, there are exceptions.

Chapter 12 A Closer Look at Writing Reports of Qualitative Research

___ 12.1 Consider using the term "qualitative" in the title or abstract of the report.

___ 12.2 In the introduction, consider discussing the choice of qualitative over quantitative methodology.

___ 12.3 Consider describing the qualitative method or approach used in the research.

___ 12.4 Consider "revealing yourself" to your reader.

___ 12.5 Avoid calling a sample "purposive" if it is really a sample of convenience.

___ 12.6 If a purposive sample was used, state the basis for the selection of participants.

___ 12.7 Consider describing how participants were recruited.

___ 12.8 Consider providing details on how the data were collected.

___ 12.9 In the results section, report quantitative results on quantitative matters.

___ 12.10 If quotations are reported, consider stating the basis for their selection.

___ 12.11 If two or more researchers participated in analyzing the data, discuss how they arrived at a consensus.

___ 12.12 Consider discussing alternative interpretations of the data and why they were rejected.

Appendix B

Thinking Straight and Writing That Way[1]

Ann Robinson
University of Arkansas at Little Rock

Everyone who submits manuscripts to top-flight journals gets rejected by the reviewers more than once in his or her publishing career. Often the rejections seem, at best, inexplicable and, at worst, biased. Rejections sting.

In a cooler moment, the disappointed author looks over the rejected paper and tries to read the reviewers' comments more calmly. What do journal reviewers look for in a manuscript? What makes a submission publishable? How can you increase the likelihood that your work will be accepted? These are good questions for any would-be author —seasoned or new—to ask.

In general, sessions on publishing "how-to's" rarely get beyond the obligatory lecture on the importance of the idea. We are told that if the idea is good, we should carry out the research study and proceed to submit the work for publication. If the how-to-get-published session gets past the point of explaining that a good study is one that asks an important question, then we are told that a publishable study is one that is reasonably free of design flaws. It seems to me that these two points ought to be considered givens. Although it is not always easy to think of a good idea, translate it into a researchable question, and design a competent study, most of us already understand the importance of these things. What we want to know now is how to increase our chances of getting competent work published.

Over the last eight years, I have developed the following questions to use when reviewing research manuscripts. They are offered as one

---

[1] Originally published in *Gifted Child Quarterly*, *32*, 367–369 as "Thinking Straight and Writing That Way: Publishing in *Gifted Child Quarterly*." Copyright 1988 by the National Association for Gifted Children. Reprinted with permission.

reviewer's "test" of the publishability of a manuscript and may be helpful as guides for the prospective author.

Reviewer Question 1: What's the point?

Early on in the first "quick read," I ask why I should be interested in this manuscript. Will this study fill a gap in the existing literature? Will this study reconcile apparently contradictory research results from studies already published? Is this study anchored to a real problem affecting the education and upbringing of children and youth? Is this study "newsworthy"? Does the author convince me in the first few paragraphs that this manuscript is going to present important information new to the field or be investigated from a fresh perspective?

The manuscripts that most effectively make their "point" often have brief introductions that state the essence of the issue in the first or last sentence of the first or second paragraph. As a reviewer, I look for that "essence of issue" sentence. It is a benchmark for clear thinking and writing.

Reviewer Question 2: Can I find the general research question?

Reviewer Question 2 is related to the first, but I am now looking for something a bit more technical. The general research question should be stated clearly, and it should serve as the lodestone for the specific questions generated for the study. Congruence is important here. If I were to take each of these specific questions and check them against the general question, I would easily see the connection. For example, in a study of the family systems of underachieving males, the general question is, "What are the interactional relationships within families of gifted students?" (Green, Fine, & Tollefson, 1988). Two specific questions derived from the general one are:

"(1) Is there a difference in the proportion of families of achieving and underachieving gifted that are classified as functional and dysfunctional? (2) Do family members having achieving or under-achieving gifted students differ in their satisfaction with their families?" (p. 268).

The manuscripts that most effectively answer Reviewer Question 2 placed the general question at the end of the review of the literature. It will be stated as a question and prefaced with a lead-in like "the general purpose of this study" or "an important research question is." Then the specific questions for the study are enumerated and set apart in a list. The

114

combination of text and visual cues makes it difficult for the reviewer to overlook the focus of the manuscript.

Reviewer Question 3: Can I get a "picture" of the subjects of this study?

The appropriate level of description for the subjects is difficult to judge. However, it is better to over- rather than underdescribe them. This is true whether the study is experimental or a naturalistic inquiry. Insufficient information about the participants in the study leaves the reviewer wondering if the conclusions are suspect. Would the results be the same if other subjects had participated? Go beyond the breakdowns by age or grade, sex, and ethnicity. If the subjects are students in a gifted program, describe the identification procedure. If the subjects are school personnel, describe their professional positions, years in service, or other variables that might affect the results. As a reviewer, I always try to determine the extent to which a subject sample is volunteer and how seriously volunteerism might bias the results. If a study is conducted in one school building, district, or one teacher or parent advocate group, I look for descriptions of this context. How large is the school or organization? Is it rural, urban, or suburban? Who is responding to surveys? Fathers or mothers? Are families intact, single parent, or extended? What is the socioeconomic level?

For example, in a study of learning styles, Ricca (1984) included the following information to give a thorough picture of the subjects.

> The study population included 425 students in grades four, five, and six from one city school and one suburban school district in Western New York. Descriptive contrast groups represented subjects who were identified as gifted and a contrast group taken from the remaining general school students available. Gifted students were identified by a multidimensional screening process with data sources indicated in Table 1 (p. 121).

This information is followed by a further explanation of the identification process and three brief tables that provide a tidy summary of student demographics and cognitive and academic characteristics. The combination of text and tables gives the reviewer a clear picture of the subjects in the study.

The reviewer may ultimately ask the author to trim the text on subjects, but over-zealous descriptions serve two purposes. First, they demonstrate to the reviewer that the author is a careful worker. Second, they rein in generalizations, which appear in the Conclusions and

Implications sections of the manuscript. An author may well be entitled to make statements about the population from which the sample of subjects is drawn, but if the demographics of the group change, the conclusions may not be safely generalized.

The manuscripts that most effectively create a picture of their sample include the basics like age, grade, sex, and ethnicity succinctly, sometimes in tabled form. Case study researchers are less likely to use tables because of smaller samples, but they do identify the reasons why they believe a subject is representative of a large group. In studies of gifted children, the most effective manuscripts clearly state the selection procedure and identify specific instruments or checklists, if appropriate, under the Subjects section of the paper.

Reviewer Question 4: Is this author killing flies with an elephant gun?

As a reviewer, I examine the manuscript for a comfortable fit among the research questions, the kinds of data that have been collected, and the tools of analysis. In the case of manuscripts that present quantitative data and statistical analyses, I apply Occam's razor. The simplest statistics are usually the best. A good research question can be insightfully investigated with relatively simple analyses provided the assumptions are not too badly violated. The purpose of statistics is to summarize and clarify, not to fog.

Of course, authors who seek to control confounded variables through the use of more sophisticated statistical treatments like the currently popular LISREL increase the likelihood that multiple causation is disentangled. We certainly gain from technological innovation; however, the key is to determine if the impetus for the study is a substantive research question or a fascination with the newest techniques.

The manuscripts that answer Reviewer Question 4 most effectively are those in which hypotheses do not sink under the weight of the analyses. As I read the Design and Analysis sections, am I able to keep my eye on the important variables? A good indicator is a sentence in the Design section that gives me the rationale for using quite sophisticated or new statistical and qualitative techniques. For example, a study of ethnic differences in a mathematics program for gifted students included the following explanation for the selection of a specialized kind of regression analysis (Robinson, Bradley, & Stanley, in review):

> Regression discontinuity is a quasi-experimental design which allows the experimenter to test for treatment effects without a randomized control group and the attendant withholding of services. This a priori design statistically controls for prior differences by using the identification variable along with program participation (status) as independent variables in a multiple regression model (p.7).

Another indication that the study is being driven by its questions rather than its statistics is the author's effort to make connecting statements between a technique and its interpretation. To return to the previous regression example:

> If the associated t-test of the regression coefficient is significant, it is indicative of a program that impacts on its participants (p. 7).

Reviewer Question 5: Would George Orwell approve?

Dogging the reviewer through both the "quick read" and the "close read" of the manuscript is the ease with which the author has answered the first four questions. If we look back at those questions, we see the common thread of clarity running through them. What is the point? Where is the question? Who is this study about? Does the analysis illuminate rather than obfuscate?

Reviewer Question 5 is the final test. Would George Orwell approve? In 1946, Orwell published "Politics and the English Language," one of the clearest statements on writing effectively ever to appear in print. The thesis of his essay was that "modern English, especially written English, is full of bad habits which spread by imitation and which can be avoided if one is willing to take the necessary trouble . . . prose consists less and less of words chosen for the sake of their meaning, and more and more of phrases tacked together like sections of a prefabricated hen-house" (p. 159). Orwell was clearly unhappy with vague writing and professional jargon. He felt that poor writing was an indication of sloppy thinking, and he excused neither the social scientist nor the novelist from his strict dicta of good, vigorous writing. He had a particular dislike of using ready-made phrases like "lay the foundation," and he was equally appalled at the indiscriminate use of scientific terms to give the impression of objectivity to biased statements.

As a reviewer, I apply Orwell's tough rules to the test of every manuscript I receive. It means that the manuscript author has answered Reviewer Questions 1 through 4 successfully.

According to Orwell, "the following rules will cover most cases:

1. Never use a metaphor, simile, or other figure of speech which you are used to seeing in print.
2. Never use a long word where a short one will do.
3. If it is possible to cut a word out, always cut it out.
4. Never use the passive where you can use the active.
5. Never use a foreign phrase, a scientific word, or a jargon word if you can think of an everyday English equivalent.
6. Break any of these rules sooner than say anything outright barbarous" (p. 170).

Orwell had the good sense to include the sixth rule as a disclaimer. All writers make errors and violate rules, sometimes out of carelessness, sometimes for effect. It is also true that writing for highly specialized journals does require the judicious use of technical language, just as sheep shearers need specialized terms to describe differing grades of wool. However, moderation in the use and the arbitrary, spontaneous creation of specialized vocabulary is certainly warranted in our field. It is refreshing to read an author who states that the subjects in the study are "thinking critically" rather than "realizing greater cognitive gains."

Orwell makes many fine points about the importance of sincerity in thinking and writing. For the prospective social science writer, none are more important than the careful selection and lively use of technical terms. I know of no more rigorous test to apply to a manuscript than to ask if George Orwell would approve. Passing this "test" means the author is thinking straight and writing that way.

References

Green, K., Fine, M. J., & Tollefson, N. (1988). Family systems characteristics and underachieving gifted adolescent males. *Gifted Child Quarterly*, *32*, 267–276.

Orwell, G. (1953*)*. Politics and the English language. In G. Orwell (Ed.)*, A Collection of Essays* (pp. 156–171). San Diego: Harcourt, Brace, Jovanovich.

Rica, J. (1984). Learning styles and preferred instructional strategies. *Gifted Child Quarterly*, *28*, 121–126.

Robinson, A., Bradley, R., & Stanley, T. D. (in review). Opportunity to achieve: The identification and performance of Black students in a program for the mathematically talented.

Appendix C

The Null Hypothesis and Significance Testing[1]

Formal significance testing begins with the *null hypothesis*. This is a statistical hypothesis that asserts that any differences we observe when studying random samples are the result of random (chance) errors created by the random sampling. For example, suppose you asked a random sample of men from some population and a random sample of women from the same population whether they support legalizing physician-assisted suicide for the terminally ill and found that 51% of the women supported it while only 48% of the men supported it. At first, you might be tempted to report that women are more supportive of this proposition than men. However, the null hypothesis warns us that the 3-percentage-point difference between women and men may have resulted solely from sampling errors. In other words, there may be no difference between men and women in the population — we may have found a difference because we administered our questionnaire to only these two particular samples.

Of course, it is also possible that the men and women in the population are truly different in their opinion on physician-assisted suicide and the population difference is responsible for the difference between the percentages for the two samples. In other words, the samples may accurately reflect the gender difference in the population. This possibility is called an *alternative hypothesis* (i.e., an alternative to the null hypothesis).

Which hypothesis is correct? It turns out that the only way to answer this question is to test the null hypothesis. If the test indicates that we may reject the null hypothesis, then we will be left with only the alternative hypothesis as an explanation. When we reject the null hypothesis, we say that we have identified a *reliable* difference — one we can rely on because it probably is not just an artifact of random errors.

Through a set of computational procedures that are beyond the scope of this book, a significance test results in a *probability that the*

---

[1] The authors are grateful to Mildred L. Patten, who wrote this appendix.

119

null hypothesis is true. The symbol for this probability is *p*. By conventional standards, when the probability that the null hypothesis is true is as low as or lower than 5 in 100, we reject the null hypothesis. (Note that a low probability means that it is unlikely that the null hypothesis is true. If something is *unlikely* to be true, we reject it as a possibility.)

The formal term that researchers use when discussing the rejection of the null hypothesis is *statistical significance*. For example, the following two statements might appear in the results section of a research report:

"The difference between the means of the liberals and conservatives is statistically significant ($p < .05$)."

"The difference between the means for the men and women is not statistically significant ($p > .05$)."

The first statement says that the probability that the null hypothesis is true is less than ($<$) 5 in 100; thus, the null hypothesis is rejected, and the difference is declared to be statistically significant. The second statement says that the probability that the null hypothesis is true is greater than ($>$) 5 in 100; thus, the null hypothesis is *not* rejected, and the difference is *not statistically significant*.

In other words, significance tests are helping us make decisions based on the odds that something is true. We all do this in everyday life. For instance, when you prepare to cross a busy street, you look at oncoming cars to judge their speed and distance to see if it is safe to cross. If you decide that there is a *low probability* that you will be able to cross the street safely, you *reject* the hypothesis that it is safe to cross the street.